A CHANGE IN THE WEATHER

The "explosive" growth of a cumulus cloud following seeding with silver iodide, August 20, 1963; (top left) 2:01 P.M. at the time the highest cloud in the center of the photograph was seeded; (top right) 2:10 P.M.; (bottom left) 2:20 P.M.; (bottom right) 2:39 P.M. (Photo credit: J. Simpson)

A CHANGE IN THE WEATHER

FITZHUGH GREEN

W · W · NORTON & COMPANY, INC · NEW YORK

Copyright © 1977 by W. W. Norton & Company, Inc. All rights reserved. Published simultaneously in Canada by George J. McLeod Limited, Toronto. Printed in the United States of America.

Library of Congress Cataloging in Publication Data

Green, Fitzhugh, 1917–
A change in the weather.

Includes index.
1. Weather control.   2. Environmental protection.
I.   Title.
QC928.G73 1977   551.5'8   77–21766
ISBN 0–393–06429–8

First Edition

1 2 3 4 5 6 7 8 9 0

FOR PENELOPE

and her teenage pals who may actually experience
answers to many of these haunting questions.

CONTENTS

ILLUSTRATIONS

PREFACE

The people of our planet are moving toward a new relationship with the environment, one which will affect our farms, our factories, our way of life, and indeed our ability to survive. This is an up-to-date report on what's happening.

At first man could only enjoy his environment when it was mild or suffer it when it was harsh. Later he began both to exploit it and to protect himself against it. From hapless nomad who gobbled up nature's bounty and moved on, he learned to farm the land and shelter himself. He fashioned tools to convert the handy resources about him into a multitudinous array of products for his comfort and amusement. He fabricated marvels of transportation over the land and water, under the sea, and into the air and outer space.

Scientists and engineers have been key figures in our long march from passive dependence on the environment to increasing dominance over it. These professionals are now experimenting with technologies that, if successful, will bring us quite a different dimension of control over our surroundings.

For example, they are experimenting with habitats sealed off from the elements. Today's Astrodome in Houston may well evolve into totally enclosed cities, safe from the vagaries of climate and from dirty air. The inventive Buckminster Fuller has explained how cities may enjoy good environmental quality under a great, airtight roof. Encapsulated dwellings may be affixed to mountainsides, under ice, or under the sea, in the search for more living space. A Princeton University physicist has a blueprint for building huge, self-sustaining satellites for colonies of adventurous scientists. Momentum toward such changes is still slight but, like the sea tide, it has begun and may come to flood sooner than we can foresee today.

Back here on earth we are approaching a degree of leverage over the environment that is so fraught with potential benefit and harm as to be almost beyond imagination. By design (as well as by accident), we have made the first moves to alter the rhythms and structure of land, sea, and atmosphere.

Programs are in progress, or under study, to modify the wasteful, destructive aspects of weather, climate, ocean currents, deserts, and earthquakes. We may soon be able to challenge such familiar sayings as "Everybody talks about the weather, but nobody does anything about it" or "climate controls our crops, but we can't control the climate".

In other words, we are attempting to improve the environment on a grand scale. At the same time, we are inadvertently putting a crimp in it. Scientists tell us that our sloppy industrial habits may already be permanently disturbing its present patterns. The result, they say, may be a new Ice Age, starting soon, or a drastic, life-snuffing warm-up of the air and oceans.

In short, we may be pushing Mother Nature toward a "change of life" that will be either helpful to humanity or catastrophic.

It seems only fair to the reader to explain how I came to write about these things. The idea emerged from United States Senator Claiborne Pell's 1974 hearings in the Senate Foreign Relations Committee, along with his proposed ban against environmental war. Witnesses showed up from all over the country; and their testimony was so—frightening—that the committee report reads like a science fiction novel: one possibility mentioned was that of an enemy's launching death-dealing tidal waves. Reading the report, I decided to find out more.

For months thereafter I dug through mountains of written material on environmental control for war and other purposes, but I found this to be a numbing experience. The writing was not only dull, but equivocal. It must be that technical journals are conjured up by magicians, for presto-chango, they can transform a heart-thumping subject like war by environment into a sleeping potion.

Then I was struck by the thought that the people who are probing into this strange area really belong to that romantic breed of hero, the explorer. Past explorers have merely pitted their physical prowess against nature. Present ones aspire to the almost god-like role of manipulating those complex geophysical forces that in the past have bent man to their will.

So I stopped reading reports for a while and got to know the intrepid individuals who are pointing the way to environmental modification. I found them fascinating and self-confident. They may hedge their points of view on the shiny, formal pages of the magazine *Science*. But if you were to hear them talk, as I have, you would feel the flame of their enthusiasm.

In the pages ahead I will describe the scientific and technological race which has already started, but whose finish can't yet be predicted.

Environmental control concerns us all. Therefore we should keep an eye on it and understand what is happening. I have tried to provide some insights.

As yet there is no ultimate expert in this burgeoning field. I certainly don't claim to be one. My interest stems from my experience in and observation of some of the organizations that must deal with it: the federal government's military, Foreign Service, and regulatory departments; the United States Senate; and a multinational corporation. In my professional experience, I have specialized in

practical ecology, oceanography, journalism, advertising, and poli-
tics.

I will recommend what should be done to speed useful changes
in our environment, as well as to avoid or soften the blows we
inflict on it.

In the hope of making things clear for the general reader (as well
as myself) I have shunned technical jargon. For those who wish to
delve deeper, the bibliography suggests a sample of the growing
body of literature.

I won't predict what will happen next, as my father once did. He
produced dozens of books on expeditions into little-known parts of
the world. So he was speaking as something of an authority when
he wrote in 1929, "Centuries may pass before man reaches the
moon."[1] Less than forty years later Neil Armstrong took his famous "giant step"!

To avoid the sins of the father, I leave precise predictions to the
reader, but offer the best information I have found, in order to
reveal the future as clearly as possible.

ACKNOWLEDGEMENTS

Oh, that mine enemy would write a book! That old chestnut certainly is fair warning to any author writing from Washington these days. Another caveat I should have been given was how much I would need to depend on friends and friendly experts. Now comes the danger of omitting mention of my gratitude to any of those who contributed their enthusiasm, and the fact and opinion so vital to the soundness of this work.

If the book misses the mark in any way it is *despite* the excellent and generous help of Robert Abel, Larry Booda, Reid Bryson, Stanley Changnon, Geryld Christianson, Pierce Corden, Joan David, Paul Dickson, Louise Duncan, Elaine Fitzback, R. Buckminster Fuller, Dolores Gregory, Kirk Harper, Tom Henderson, Wilmot Hess, Linda Hilwig, Joseph Knox, Rear Admiral Gene La Rocque (Ret.), Noel La Seur, Ronald La Voie, Gordon J. F. MacDonald, Lester Machta, Michael MacCracken, Robert J. McManus, J. Murray Mitchell, Jr., Michael Mulcahy, Stewart B. Nelson, Donald Oakley, Senator Claiborne Pell, James Petersen,

Steuart Pittman, Herbert Quinn, Pierre St. Amand, Vincent J. Schaefer, Joanne Simpson, Robert Simpson, S. Fred Singer, George Sisson, Joseph Smagorinsky, Athelstan Spilhaus, Harris B. Stewart, Jr., Walter E. Strope, Wilson Talley, Edward Teller, Peter Thacher, Jack Thompson, William von Arx, Bernard Vonnegut, Edith Brown Weiss, Robert White, Howard Wilcox, Burke Wilkinson, Merlin Williams, Herbert Wiser, Mary Yates, and Charles Zracket.

I want especially to thank Madeleine (Bibi) McKeon for exceptional valor and intelligence in research and in the mechanics of assembling this book. Her unfailing, unstinting support was crucial to its completion.

PART ONE

ENVIRONMENTAL MODIFICATION: POSITIVE

1

CLOUD SURGERY TO MAKE RAIN

We humans may soon be able to change the weather at our whim. Not always, but sometimes.

How did we arrive at this astounding ability? Before I started my inquiry, I thought we had achieved it only recently. Except for the rain dances of the American Indian, I was aware of no efforts to cajole the gods or the elements themselves into obeying our wishes. I was wrong.

Two thousand years ago Plutarch thought his contemporaries might already be modifying weather, by accident. He noted that "extraordinary rains pretty generally fall after a great battle."[1] Others in history also spotted this phenomenon, thinking it due to noise, especially after the invention of gunpowder. In World War II gases from munitions factories (and since then, nuclear explosions) were thought to affect local and global weather.

Even as early as 1839 people were trying to create do-it-yourself weather. That was the year James P. Espy said that if large enough outside fires were lit they would create updrafts, thus causing cumulus clouds likely to bring rain. But no one tested Espy's scheme for 115 years. Then in France and Africa some informal trials were run and some rain ensued.

After the Civil War Edward Power's book *War and Weather* recorded numerous occasions where the gunfire exchanges were followed by rain.[2] Powers was convinced that he knew how to make rain with a "big bang": he, too, may have read what Plutarch wrote about the battle-rain sequence. Finally, the United States Department of Agriculture's forestry division responded to pressures from Congress and others who believed Powers. Tests were conducted to see if explosives would make "airquakes" resulting in rain. The outcome was fuzzy. But the publicity given the experiments opened the way in 1893 for a "rash of rainmakers who, armed with crude pyrotechnics and a convincing sales pitch, became a conspicuous part of the American rural scene plying their questionable trade for a decade or more."[3]

In Europe, superstition and good luck tokens were used. Determined to ward off hailstones as if they were evil spirits, the Italians tried everything but the kitchen stove: exorcism, ritual fires, anti-hail brooms, "aerostats" hoisted to discharge the clouds' electricity, church-bell ringing and wide-bore cannons.

In 1924 an American, Dr. E. Leon Chaffee, flew through clear air at altitudes of 5,000 feet to 10,000 feet and bombarded the clouds beneath with shovelfuls of sand. He claimed that after this treatment, the clouds vanished.

In the 1930s Henry C. L. Houghton of the Massachusetts Institute of Technology thought that spraying water-absorptive material such as common salt into fogs might disperse them. His attempt to do this was partly successful.

In 1938 two optimistic Hungarians, Gorog and Rovo, ladled oil on a lake and ignited it, thus sending up a plume of hot air which they hoped would bring rain. They reported that it did. But they didn't mention that the precipitation might have been a bit sooty with partly consumed hydrocarbons, which it doubtless was.

Since that time Swedes and Americans have experimented with

the burning of oil spills as a way of getting rid of such messes. The trouble is that oil on water often won't burn, particularly when the wind is blowing and the waves curl and break. The U.S. Coast Guard knows this, but (urged by Senator Claiborne Pell who is a captain in the Coast Guard Reserve) grudgingly tested a "wicking agent" in the seven-million-gallon oil spill of the tanker *Argo Merchant* on Nantucket Shoal in 1976. A wicking agent draws oil to the top of the water, where it is exposed to the air and where combustion can therefore occur; it embodies the same principle as the wick in a candle. But the rough seas around the *Argo Merchant* spill stirred the number six fuel oil into an emulsion with salt water (it's a myth that oil and water don't mix!) and the Coast Guard demonstrated by two tests in the spilled oil that burning was unfeasible under such conditions. When floating oil does catch fire, its black smoke tends to return to earth as dirty rain, which soils windows, crops, automobiles, clean clothes—everything it touches.

After World War II, individuals and their governments picked up the pace to lasso and corral nature's maverick—the weather. Since then, several countries, particularly the United States, Great Britain, the Soviet Union, South Africa, Switzerland, and Australia, have been trying to augment nature's rain and snowfall, cut the damage from hail, subdue hurricanes, tame tornadoes, disperse fog, and reduce lightning.

These goals are ambitious and difficult, but efforts are continuing and so are the claims of success and the counterclaims of failure. Where does the truth lie? The weather, and whether we can one day manage it, is important to all of us.

Most modern attempts at weather control focus on the cloud, which, speaking unromantically, is simply a visible mass of mist or ice particles suspended in the air. The cloud forms a key part of the energy exchange between sun, sea, earth, and atmosphere that powers the world's weather system.

However, the weather is so complicated that the finest scientists still can't explain it or accurately foretell its doings except in localized areas and for a few hours or a day or two at a time. It contains so many interrelated elements that it is difficult even to name them all.

As soon as I realized this fact I wondered how I was going to write about the meteorological riddle that baffles the best-trained brains in the field. Books help us generalists to understand things—even the dry tomes of science. But just as a tenderfoot tourist in the Canadian woods needs a guide, I had to have pathfinders to keep me on track. Fortunately the scientific woods in the United States are full of friendly meteorologists, and they are a helpful lot. I expected my naive and ignorant questioning might be rebuffed by intellectual snobbery. On the contrary, these talented sages of science proved to be patient, and also extremely articulate.

This should not surprise anyone: There are two reasons why the meteorologists can explain things so well. First, they all give lectures, and many teach in universities at the graduate level. Second, many of them have developed theories on weather and climate which they persistently plug, in public and among their peers.

Where does one look for such guides? They abound, of course, in the nationwide empire of the National Oceanic and Atmospheric Administration (part of the United States Department of Commerce), known as NOAA.* I have traveled to see NOAA people in Miami; Rockville, Maryland (NOAA headquarters); Princeton; and Boulder, Colorado. Their names will emerge as their thoughts appear, along with those of other independent, academic, or government experts I have visited or telephoned around the country.

On the intricacies of the weather system I started my quizzing with youthful Michael MacCracken, a top climatologist. He is on the staff of Dr. Joseph Knox, director of atmospheric sciences in

---

* Pronounced "Noah." Since NOAA is to oceans what the United States National Air and Space Administration (NASA) is to space, its architects originally dubbed it the "wet NASA."

the University of California's Lawrence Livermore Laboratory, which, along with Los Alamos, houses the nation's nuclear weapons research. This work is funded by the Energy Research and Development Agency in Washington.

Dr. MacCracken said he wants to simplify the workings of the weather system by reducing it to a mathematical model. He explained that to do this he would like to put all the data representing the dynamics of the atmosphere and the ocean into Livermore's multimillion-dollar computer—one of the most sophisticated, advanced to date. He said this mathematical model should be the one way we crystal-ball the interactions between sea and air which form the core mechanism of weather.

What would you learn? I asked the young scientist. "Nothing," he laughed, "because even our computer can't swallow, much less digest, such a rich meal of information." Actually, I later found out, this combination modeling of oceans and atmosphere is in progress at NOAA's geophysical lab at Princeton, although its form is still too simplistic to provide dependable insights. In other words, to reduce the problem to understandably simple terms details have to be omitted which tend to make the answers incomplete.

Happily, despite the formidable complexity of global weather, man has actually begun not only to induce rain, but other near miracles of local weather change.

However, this is a field of technology that is still barely emergent, and the enthusiasm of some of its practitioners tends to blur the facts: It is hard to distinguish their hopes and beliefs from what they've actually accomplished.

Freeze a Cloud to Make Rain and Snow

The new day in weather modification dawned in July 1946, heralded by an artificial cloud that was the creation of three able men: Irving Langmuir, a Nobel laureate chemist; his junior researcher, technician Vincent J. Schaefer; and a physical chemist and meteorologist named Bernard Vonnegut. All were General Electric employees tackling the mystery of precipitation.

Schaefer took the first, historic step toward ever-ready rainmaking for mankind. He and Langmuir were trying to see how a cold cloud, heavy with water vapor, produces rain or snow. They had made observations, for example, on the cloud-shrouded top of Mount Washington, New Hampshire. There they noted that the reason for rime forming on everything exposed to the weather appeared to be a certain combination of humidity and temperature.

What if there were only the cold cloud, without the mountain peak? Would that automatically mean snow would form? Such questions percolated in Schaefer's head until one day he decided to assemble an artificial setting with propitious "weather" conditions. To do so economically, he looked around for something on hand that might be adapted. This he found in the deep-freeze unit of a GE refrigerator on the market that year. This chamber measured about four feet on a side. He placed it in his laboratory and lined it with black velvet, for visibility in case the experiment he planned should actually trigger some precipitation. Then he plugged in the cord and turned on the deep-freeze machine. When the temperature in the box dropped well below 32°F, he exhaled a deep sigh into it. By electric light, he watched his breath become a small cloud; but no precipitation resulted.

Since it was a hot day, he decided to cool the freezer still further, and dropped in a fist-size block of solid carbon dioxide—known as dry ice—with a temperature of −112°F. Magically, a beautiful little snowstorm appeared, its delicate flakes landing gently on the black velvet. Evidently the temperature of the "human cloud" (Schaefer's breath), which had dropped to about −40°F, was a critical factor.

Tingling with anticipation, Schaefer wrote up the event and plunged into plans to repeat it in a *real* cloud.

On November 13, 1946, he commandeered a plane and had it flown into a flat, thick stratus cloud near Schenectady, New York.

For about a half mile, he hand-scattered out the window of the slow-moving propeller craft bits of crushed dry ice—about three pounds in all. Then he told Curt Talbot, the pilot, to circle back under the cloud where he had just "seeded" it. *Mirabile dictu!* Graceful curtains of lace-white snow fell 2,000 feet below the cloud, and then evaporated. Schaefer's exultation is recorded in his notebook: "While still in the cloud, as we saw the glinting crystals all over, I turned to Curt and we shook hands and I said, 'We did it!' "[4]

Langmuir was so pleased at Schaefer's feat he promptly told the world that rain-making had arrived. Certainly, he claimed, we have learned how to freeze a cloud to make snow. How unusual, in this often selfish species! The noble Langmuir clearly was untroubled by jealousy at his understudy's having copped what might have been his own greatest achievement. Langmuir, by then about sixty, treated his twentyish assistant like a favorite son. In fact, the two were friends who shared an interest in outdoor life and frequently hiked the hills together.

Meanwhile, their colleague, Vonnegut (brother of widely read writer Kurt Vonnegut, Jr.) was searching for the particle around which water vapor could collect (nucleate) and precipitate at a temperature near $0°C$ ($32°F$), the normal temperature for freezing. Earlier, quite a few Europeans had been theorizing on how clouds dissolve into rain—A. Wegener in 1911, Tor Bergeron in 1933, W. Findeisen in 1938, and Peppler in 1940. But Vonnegut, Langmuir, and Schaefer were working independently and more inventively.

Using the same kind of refrigerator that Schaefer had selected, Vonnegut produced his own meteorological trigger: After breathing into the glacial chamber to form a fake cloud, he tossed in a twenty-five cent coin, which instantly catalyzed a tiny snow flurry. But when he tried again days later, in an identical unit, nothing happened.

Being a careful scientist, Vonnegut chemically analyzed the velvet and the original chamber for other substances that might be present. Sure enough, there were traces of iodide. That, combined with the silver in the quarter, made silver iodide, Vonnegut reasoned. He repeated the experiment, this time directly dusting in particles of the compound. It brought snow, not only in the box but also, later, in a sky cloud. The idea of using silver iodide was not really coincidental: Vonnegut had observed that the structure of silver iodide crystals closely resembles that of ice crystals.

Now the three men were ecstatic with their marvelous new power to freeze a cloud and make it rain. In simplest terms, what they were doing with dry ice was to congeal water vapor; and with the silver iodide they were providing a nucleus for supercooled water vapor to stick to and become ice.

Seeding a cloud with dry ice or silver iodide sounds easy to do, and it is; but it doesn't always bring rain. It sounds easy to understand, but even topflight meteorologists can't completely explain why it works when it does, or vice versa. Nor can they do much more than describe the actual phenomenon: When water vapor flowers into ice crystals as a result of seeding, not just a few crystals appear, but hundreds of thousands—instantaneously—so a few pounds of silver iodide may precipitate thousands of gallons of rainwater from a single cloud.

In a word, much ignorance remains, thirty years after Schaefer's dramatic breakthrough. Yet, until Langmuir died in 1959, he wrote and spoke enthusiastically that rainmaking had really arrived. News media picked up his lead: "Man's trouble with drought is just about over!" Farmers and state governments in dry areas became believers; and still pay hard dollars to private seeding firms to increase moisture for their crops. So do foreign governments, if they can afford to.

Why, then, is drought an ever-growing problem, both at home and abroad? Were Schaefer, Langmuir, and Vonnegut meteorological dreamers who deluded themselves and the public? Are the "rainmakers" who sell their services today taking money fraudulently? The answer is mainly no, but with qualifications.

Langmuir's claims were premature and excessive, although

Schaefer defends himself and Langmuir to this day. One of his arguments is a series of photographs that depict the holes in clouds that are cut by seeding. I have heard Schaefer lecture and seen him show a slide that pictures an L-shaped trench in the clouds, thousands of feet long. "If they [his superiors at General Electric] hadn't admitted what we had done to that cloud," he jokes now, "I'd have printed a giant GE up there!"

Schaefer and his followers have often produced data to record a rise in rainfall after seeding. So the question is usually not a matter of scientific veracity, but of incomplete knowledge about a very complicated slice of the world—its atmosphere. Nevertheless, there are a few deliberate quacks who mislead the public. Vincent Schaefer, now a pleasant, white-thatched, healthy hulk of a man in his late sixties, is not one of them. He and Vonnegut, a tall, slender, modest, and quiet scientist with a dark block of a mustache, are still greatly respected, not only for their original discoveries but for their continuing quest for more truth on the subject in the years since their first experiments.

Despite all the fanfare in 1946, the government's early response to cloud seeding was negative. To begin with, experts of the Weather Bureau (a part of the Department of Commerce) rejected the reports of Schaefer, Langmuir, and Vonnegut as unproven scientifically. They argued that an experienced weather watcher can usually tell by looking at a cloud whether it is about to produce rain or snow. So if he seeds it and rain or snow follows, no one can tell whether the precipitation was caused by seeding, or in nature. Nevertheless, the 1946 discovery has stimulated various branches of our federal government to investigate the possibility of "cloud surgery" off and on to this very day.

Although at first they criticized Langmuir and the others for their inability to verify claims, government scientists have since tried to get around this difficulty. To do so they have adapted the technique of "randomization." This is a control procedure which prevents a scientist from letting his personal bias on a subject influence the results of his experiment. In cloud-seeding tests randomization is accomplished by keeping the researcher who flies through a cumulus cloud and activates the plane's seeding mechanism from knowing whether he is shooting silver iodide salts or a blank.

I should explain that most of our Government's experimental seeding is now done by pyrotechnics. These are cartridges which when ignited emit the seeding agent as smoke. NOAA's meteorologists have been using them for some years in the Florida Area Cumulus Experiment (FACE). This has been one of the government's most significant pursuits of the will-o'-the-wisp of rainmaking.

In 1976 I visited the Miami base of this important project. There I observed that the silver iodide is mixed with explosive powder and put in small flare cartridges; the flares are about 5 inches long, with a diameter of 1½ inches. Packaged in cardboard, the flares are fired individually, by electronic control, from steel barrels set in racks under the plane—100 to 200 flares are loaded in each plane. The flares burn out totally after about a 4,000-foot drop, so there is no danger of hurting anyone on the ground. (This is an improvement over past practice: When the scientists first tested pyrotechnic seeding they had to do it over the sea, because rockets they used then did not consume themselves—and woe to any innocent who was standing beneath.

In randomized experimental flights two types of flares are used—one with silver iodide, and one without it (like a placebo). From inside the plane both sound alike when fired.

Literally the researcher flies under "sealed orders." Without his knowledge, a pattern is set in advance by randomization, specifying the days during, let's say, a month of experimentation on which the flares will contain silver iodide and the days on which they will be merely "placebos." Every day that flights are made, whether or not seeding occurs, pictures are taken and data collected and later examined to see what results, if any, occurred when the plane passed through a cloud. At that time, the reporting scientist is let in on the secret of which days were the seeding days.

Research since 1946 has been done first by a combination of

private universities with support from the National Science Foundation; by the Commerce Department, for the past ten years or so, under Dr. Robert White, saturnine-faced, hard-driving, capable administrator of NOAA; and by the navy, the air force, and the Bureau of Reclamation in the Department of the Interior. In 1976 a total of nine government agencies ran weather modification programs.

Inexplicably, the Department of Agriculture has hung back from any sizeable support of weather modification. It would seem logical that the government's agricultural experts would have the greatest interest in efforts to improve the weather upon which crops depend; but logic is not always king in Washington.

Schaefer did his research out of personal curiosity and, as he says, pretty much on his own. "If we'd tried to clear with managment [General Electric] what we had in mind, we'd probably never have got anything accomplished," he chuckles in today's spirit of "up the organization."

The U.S. government and other governments, plus private, commercial and academic outfits, have tried to evolve principles of rainmaking in diverse ways—for example, by releasing hot, silver-iodide-laden smoke from ground dispensers, letting it rise into the clouds. This method saves the expense of an airplane, but it lacks dependability as a delivery system, because of shifting winds, temperature, and humidity.

Another approach is to concentrate on "orographic" clouds. A cloud of this type picks up moisture and then is blown up the side of a mountain. As it rises, it cools to the point where seeding will usually turn on the snow or rain faucet.

On the western slope of the Rockies, winds from the Pacific form these orographic clouds. A Claifornia utility company, Pacific Gas and Electric, has for twenty-five years hired commercial seeders to augment winter snowfall—"snowpack," it's called—and hence the spring runoff of needed water. The results have been positive, with increases in snowfall of at least 10 percent, and the most dependable of the artifically induced precipitation to date.

Cumulus clouds are the white, fleecy, billowy types that form around noon, after the sun has heated up the land and water during the morning. Evaporate from lakes, rivers, streams, oceans, or even wet grass rises with the air heated by solar radiation hitting these surfaces.

There was a man in England who made a lot of money betting he could make a cumulus cloud disappear simply by looking at it. His trick is an old one to meteorologists. Although on a fair day clouds appear as motionless as grazing cattle, the cumulus variety lives a fast, volatile life, which usually ends in a few minutes to an hour, although the big ones may last several hours.

NOAA has since 1963 operated the Florida Area Cumulus Experiment to study cumulus clouds because they are the most likely to gestate into rainers. In 1976 FACE's first phase was completed with positively encouraging results. I watched it myself and enjoyed riding a rainmaker plane and all the preparations that go with it.

Each day's exercise starts with a briefing at the computer center building of the University of Miami. A group of some twenty scientists, engineers, radar experts, contract airplane pilots, and student interns listen attentively as the plan for the day is laid out by the FACE director, Dr. William Woodley—a cheerful, vibrant young leader.

In the audience I note a tall, graceful blonde woman of middle years. She follows the proceedings closely. Her name is Dr. Joanne Simpson. Dr. Woodley is a former student of hers and she at the moment is a consultant on his team.

Dr. Simpson was the first woman meteorologist to win a Ph.D. in this country. She was "allowed" to study weather because of the manpower shortage during World War II.

She did marry and have three children but has also kept to meteorology ever since. So well, in fact, that she has risen to be a renowned authority, author, professional research leader, and international commercial consultant in the growing science of cloud physics and control. All these trappings of accomplishment have not dimmed the delightful sense of wonderment she exudes.

Dr. Simpson in 1963 launched an idea that, after Schaefer's discovery, has become a second major benchmark toward bringing rain from clouds. She calls the rainmaking process originated by Schaefer a "static" means of augmenting rain, since it doesn't involve movement or changes of the cloud. Dr. Simpson names hers the "dynamic" theory; she and her husband, Robert, a hurricane expert, field-tested it in 1963, with exciting results. (See frontispiece—the August 20, 1963, "exploding seeded cloud.")

What they wanted to do, and did, was to make a cloud grow, in the hope that if a small cloud gives a small amount of rain, a large one will give commensurately more.

The theory is based on the principle that when water vapor condenses into water or ice, it gives up heat (the solar heat absorbed when the water evaporated, known as "latent heat of evaporation"). Therefore, opined the Simpsons, if we release trillions of microscopic particles of silver iodide which then match up with a like number of water vapor particles, lots of heat will be released. Heated, the cloud will become buoyant and will expand upwards and outwards. The top side will reach high altitudes, where the temperature will lower to around $-14°F$; ice crystals will form; and they will reach the ground as rain—plenty of it. But not every time.

In Miami the hour-long FACE briefing comes to a close. A meteorologist has given the latest weather conditions in the FACE area—about 5,000 square miles of southern Florida, in a rough quadrilateral including Miami. Satellite and local observations confirm that this should be a fruitful day for cloud seeding. The high-pressure lid is gone. This is good, because for a week it has stunted the growth of promising little cumulus clouds.

Woodley and aides speed almost recklessly through heavy traffic—twenty minutes of it—to the airport. He doesn't want to waste plane time. NOAA has chartered three planes with three pilots each for three months for FACE 1976. The cost, $205,000, is modest compared to the alternative of NOAA's owning and operating their own planes.

The planes are tagged "CU 1," "CU 2," and "CU 3." Woodley

tells us they used to be called "Seeder" 1, 2, and 3, but the names were changed to avoid stirring up Florida residents. People are very jumpy about rainmaking activity, it seems, and rumors, bad publicity, and panic are possible if, for example, they hear on citizen band radio the talk between Seeder 1 and its base. This psychological resistance to any kind of weather modification is rather widespread. It will endure and probably increase as the tempo of research and practice heightens. A great deal must be learned and shared with the public before weather modification becomes accepted as "safe."

Before leaving, Dr. Woodley and Dr. Simpson don pastel green flying suits with "NOAA" stenciled in black over the chest. The pilots and copilots of CU 1 and CU 2 meet them in a tiny ready room, put the blindfolds on them, and lead them to the two twin-engined, nine-seater Piper Navajos waiting on the tarmac. The reason for the blindfolds is that a mistake has been made by the flare manufacturers: they have color-marked the real seeders and the placebos differently, so that a look at the rack under the plane will reveal whether or not this is to be a "seeding" day.

CU 1 and CU 2, carrying Woodley and Simpson, respectively, take off; but big, tourist-laden jets crowd them down below seeding height for several minutes. Woodley is disappointed. He may be on the verge of vital discovery.

At last the clearances come for the planes to rise and head for the northwest corner of the experimental area. Woodley's radar monitor, back in his office, steadily scans the total area and can locate clouds that have rain potential. The monitor has spotted two small cumulus towers that seem to have a large amount of moisture in them. Soon Woodley and Simpson confirm this visually.

Each plane has a still camera mounted forward that takes photos every two seconds. CU 1 has a moving picture camera to record seeding passes at clouds. Each plane also has a large electronic box giving readouts from the wing sensors showing temperature, humidity, wind speed, and other atmospheric conditions.

CU 1 and CU 2 approach the two junior-sized targets. Their altitude is about 19,000 feet and the ambient temperature reads −14°F. The planes fly through them, one through each cloud. Inside the clouds, the aircraft instantly are carried fast and smoothly upward, as in an elevator of the Empire State Building. A good sign, notes Woodley: a strong updraft like this is important for seeding.

The planes circle, and this time Woodley and Simpson fire the flares as they enter the clouds. Each fires six times. That means some 700 trillion particles of silver iodide have poured into the two clouds.

The planes withdraw, and the scientists watch what ensues. After five minutes they begin to see the two clouds swelling and stretching. Woodley's radar monitor tells him by radio that rain shadows in the clouds are now visible. In a half hour they have merged. After an hour the single giant anvil-topped cumulonimbus has swollen to over 40,000 feet in height and its base near the ground has fattened to over 500 square miles! The former fleecy whiteness has darkened to an angry gray-black, now intermittently shot with jagged sticks of lightning.

This monster cloud system, which mushroomed so fast from single seeding of two isolated cumuli, dumped a huge volume of rain. In the distance Woodley's office radarscope was recording the event. Drs. Simpson's and Woodley's 1968 experiments showed that single cloud seedings can result in 100 to 150 acre-feet per cloud more than untouched clouds. (A acre-foot is a way of measuring water supply: It means simply an acre of water, one foot deep.) Taking their 1968 and 1970 experiments together, they estimated the seeding effect to result in more than three times as much water as the unseeded clouds.

The planes land and the scientists nod happily to each other, although neither is sure whether the explosive sequence they've just witnessed stemmed from seeding or from natural causes. In fact, they won't know until the summer's schedule is complete whether they actually seeded the clouds. The fact is they did, and the day is a tremendous success.

Dr. Woodley and his crew care strongly about their airborne experimentation. I could see how deeply they are motivated on the day I flew with them on a less fortunate mission. Because of a "temperature inversion" in the air, the budding cumulus clouds flattened or decapitated themselves on the cold roof above them, and their promise as rain-bearers was aborted, as was our flight.

Dr. Simpson is optimistic about this research; its implications include more than merely the augmentation of natural rain. If we can control one aspect of cumulus activity, why not others, in the future? Since cumulus clouds fuel large wind systems, drive storms, and control the exchange of radiant energy from the sun, the ability to alter cumuli may lead to control of storm and weather patterns. Larger-scale weather and climate modification—once only a dream of science fiction—may soon be on our horizon. Dr. Simpson is a professional. I share her cautious optimism.

Squeeze a Cloud

Thus far I've tried to share my findings on how to make a cloud precipitate by forcing crystallization of water particles by super-cooling the clouds. Rain results when the emerging snow or ice melts on the way down to the earth's surface.

I'm sure that on a hot summer day the reader would wonder, as I have, whether warm clouds give rain, too. They do, though in a different way. What happens is that as the air grows denser with moisture, the vapor collects on microscopic particles, or nuclei, in the atmosphere; and the resultant individual droplets begin to enlarge as the cloud nears total saturation—100 percent humidity. This occurs at what is known to sailors and farmers as the "dew point"—the temperature at which a vapor begins to condense. As the little water drops grow they begin to fall, and as they fall they hit and combine with other drops in a process called "collision and coalescence." This means that the drops snowball in size until they reach a half millimeter or more in diameter—big enough to fall earthward. That is when the first heavy drop bloops onto the top of your nose, or the back of your hand. For reasons not entirely clear, collision and coalescence starts with only a few raindrops, but then the same phenomenon racks the whole cloud in a paroxysm, and the cloud empties itself in a shower.

Lately some researchers have managed to squeeze more rain out of a warm cloud by spraying it with water from a fog nozzle or with a powder of chemical salts; even table salt (sodium choloride) gives good results. This method does not cause a heavier downpour, but the rainfall can be prolonged by squirting the cloud before the rainfall starts and after it begins to dwindle. The use of salts is easier than using the water spray, because the volume needed is considerably less. However, salt is corrosive; so now the scientists are injecting the clouds with safer chemicals, such as urea. They have also graduated to the more sophisticated method of putting the chemicals in capsules, which melt and release their contents (like cold pills) according to a predetermined timing.

Warm clouds generally present a less satisfactory target than cold ones, but they have to be used if there is a drought and there are no other clouds in the sky.

This is how rainmaking has advanced from tribal rituals and prayers to an imperfect but real development in modern technology. Using the principles involved, we've also learned other types of useful cloud surgery.

2

CLOUD SURGERY TO MODERATE FOUL WEATHER AND TO MAKE A PROFIT

As cloud seeding has grown more respectable, scientists and entrepreneurs have begun to apply it to the control of bad weather: clouds, fog, tornadoes, lightning, hurricanes, and hail. My *tour d'horizon* of these new efforts has showed me some promising prospects, despite caveats from scientific purists and pessimists.

Cloud Dispersal

As the search for more energy intensifies, solar power looks more attractive. But the sun is not always faithful. At least a quarter of the eastern United States on any given day suffers a gray-out from decks of stratus clouds. These make up a flat, thick cloud layer that blots out the sun and messes up the efficiency of sun ray collectors. It would be wonderful if we could simply eliminate clouds when we don't need them for rain.

We can now get rid of clouds under certain conditions. Experiments with clouds at the supercooled layer proved this, way back in 1948. The General Electric Company, in collaboration with the federal government, ran a series of tests called Project Cirrus that had a spectacular outcome. One day dry ice scattered from a plane at the rate of only about a pound per mile cleared out a Y-shaped track fifty-seven miles long and nearly two miles wide.

Similar experiments in other countries brought similar results, producing two-mile-wide clear-ups within a half hour of seeding, according to B. J. Mason, the British expert. Cloud decks about 3,000 feet thick would disappear if seeded at the rate of between one and ten pounds of dry ice per mile, Mason reported: "When clouds only 500 ft in depth were seeded only about 10 min elapsed before the ground could be seen, but for depths of 2000 ft this time was increased to about 25 min."[1]

The trouble with this system for cloud removal is that new clouds form in the openings. Mason said that in the Project Cirrus trial the openings were half-filled in two hours, though some see-through spots were still visible after four hours. Obviously if cloud dispersal is done in order to permit solar energy to be tapped, seeding will have to be repeated every hour or so all day, given the same conditions that prevailed during Project Cirrus.

Ground generators, also, can destroy clouds. They emit hot smoke containing silver iodide particles, which moves upward into the cloud by convection. Seeding via these smoke makers costs far less than by seeding from an airplane aloft, especially in terms of energy, unless surface wind currents interfere.

Fog Dispersal

Fog—that soundless, malevolent enemy—regularly makes landing fields, sea lanes, and the New Jersey Turnpike into traps of death and damage. Fog joined the Nazi forces at Bastogne and delayed the end of World War II by grounding the Allied fighter planes for a week or more, thus permitting the Nazis their final mass offensive—one which very nearly succeeded.

Despite the fabulous advances of radar, radio, and other electronic instrumentation, fog still slows up and slops up transportation of all kinds. Perhaps the reader has undergone (as I have) the ordeal of skippering a sailboat in the summer fogs of New England's offshore waters. Mole-blind in these circumstances, I have found my way into port relying mainly on a fathometer (depth finder) to avoid dramatic confrontations with the land.

Also, like the clouds, fog intercepts the sun's rays on their way to solving our energy shortage. "It's an ill wind that blows nobody good" does not apply to fog—at least in peacetime. Can we free ourselves of this recurrent pest? The answer is a foggy yes—to some extent.

In fact, attempts to eradicate fog have been made over a longer period than has the seeding of clouds to bring rain, and with better effect. Warren Beckwith, United Airlines's able meteorologist, gave me the background. It began with some Dutch fog seeding with dry ice back in 1930. Results? So-so. During World War II, although we Allies couldn't remove the mists over the Battle of the Bulge, we sometimes succeeded in temporarily clearing airfields by burning gasoline in ditches along runways. This technique saved many pilots who returned from missions and ran into fog that had rolled in during their absence.

After the war, the trio Schaefer, Vonnegut, and Langmuir briefly turned their attention to fog dispersal, without any noteworthy accomplishments. In 1949 local cloud seeders were acclaimed for freeing fogbound Medford, Oregon. They thinned the fog just long enough to allow some emergency medical cases to be airlifted out of Medford to better hospitals elsewhere.

Later, some ex-navy pilots pumped hot brine (containing sodium chloride) through an airplane's exhaust stack to cut away clouds; however, as I said earlier, salt is corrosive and harmful to machinery and buildings, so this was not an acceptable method.

Finally, in 1962, dry-ice seeding of cold fog began on a commercial basis and has now become a standard procedure for twelve airports in the United States that are often fog-locked. That and other new kinds of fog removal have become so dependable that forty or fifty airports use them regularly in various nations around the world.

Warm fog is not so obedient, but there are widespread attempts to coax it under control too. The French at least were able to remove the thick fogs at Orly Airport, both cold and warm, by burning liquid propane in ground generators; this treatment simply dries up the fog. In one frightful pea-souper that disrupted all traffic, airport personnel stood jet plane engines along the runways to warm the air and evaporate the fog. Now they've perfected the technique: they burn propane underground and lead the heat to the field through metal ducts.

Ground level combustion of liquid propane operated by remote control is growing in popularity in the United States. Additionally, helicopters flying overhead literally blow away the fog by brute force. The United States Air Force often did this in Vietnam to speed up evacuation of the battle wounded.

An unexpected cure turned up one day at Seattle-Tacoma Airport, where the entire field was suddenly enshrouded by fog; a half hour later it was pushed back to the edges of the runways. The exhausts of waiting planes had blow-dried the hanging mist!

Since 1962, United States antifog research in many quarters—particularly in the air force and navy, the universities, and the airlines—has amounted to only about $2.5 million. Nevertheless, Mr. Beckwith told me, industry has benefited from artificial fog dispersal to the tune of some 4,800 landings and takeoffs plus 210,000 passenger trips that would not have been possible otherwise, as well as some $5 million to $7 million not lost by airlines in operating costs. The Federal Aviation Administration has estimated a total saving to passengers of anywhere from $7 million to $50 million in this period. This record is encouraging, and suggests that more research might yield even better results. Although instrument landings can be made with low ceilings, actual ground-hugging fog still will close most airfields tight shut.

Hail Reduction

Every year hailstorms ruin a billion dollars worth of crops. Hail slams down on farmland like a bombardment from heaven, with stones reaching diameters of up to six inches. It has buffeted tobacco fields, vineyards, and other vulnerable plantings in the United States, Africa, Asia and Europe.

The Soviets, with their heavy dependence on agriculture, have fought back against destructive hail. They fire lead and silver iodide pellets from giant rifles and rockets to diminish the size of hailstones. They report such victorious results that in the United States the National Center for Atmospheric Research (NCAR) decided to experiment with the USSR's techniques. NCAR's research has been extensive, but so far inconclusive.

The purpose of introducing silver iodide is to build up competing hailstone embryos in a hail-bearing cloud to create more stones of smaller sizes so they'll do less damage to the "target field" below, or may be small enough to melt into rain before landing.

A trinational study (Italy, France, Switzerland) in Switzerland is examining the Russian experience. The three nations bought the Soviet rockets for the research. An American meteorologist told me, in confidence, that the Soviets requested the results be kept private in case it proves that their glowing reports were exaggerated.

If we can validate hail reduction methods, then we can save nearly a billion dollars annually in damage. Even if the research results are negative a lot of farms will save the money they pay to commercial cloud seeders.

The Business of Cloud Seeding

In the years since research in cloud modification began, individuals and organizations have been peddling the new technology for profit. They charge farmers, utility companies, and county and state governments for flying through clouds and seeding them to reduce hail and increase rainfall or snowpack which melts into useable runoff in the spring—and which the West needed so badly in the winter of 1966–67. Sometimes they inseminate the clouds with ground generators.

Actually, seeding services are sold at bargain rates. Vast acreage can be treasted with relatively small amounts of silver iodide or dry ice and the seeders don't make more than a few percent above costs. Despite the uncertain provability of weather modification, farmers feel that even long odds on having rain or protection against hail are worthwhile. Accordingly they contract for seeding, either one by one or in co-op purchases for several farms at a time.

Irving Krick has been called the Midas of weather modification ("weather mod"). At one time he is said to have had half of Oklahoma under contract for seeding, besides doing some weather forecasting. Krick's reputation took wing during World War II when he was a crack Army meteorologist.

Tom Henderson is another prosperous operator. He sets up a nonstop hail watch on his customer's property and strikes only when he spots an actual hailstorm building. For months at a time he conducts continuous twenty-four-hour monitoring of clouds overhead, by radar and eyeball. Simultaneously he keeps two or three planes and pilots standing by for action. These can be called to take off and attack—like a swarm of irritated bees—any cloud that looks hailworthy.

A Texas farmer named Bryant says he and his cooperative have been buying Henderson's hail protection at $1 per acre for six years now.

"Are you satisfied?" I asked.

"Sure are," said Bryant, "before Henderson the average hail storm would leave a foot-and-a-half blanket of marble-sized stones. Now we seldom see any hail big enough to hurt our corn and soybeans. He's so good we plan to buy some rainmaking for him soon."

Pacific Gas and Electric and Southern California Edison are also satisfied customers. They've been hiring commercial seeders for more than twenty-five years, since 1951, so they must like what they get. Bill Hess, who directs NOAA's Environmental Research Laboratories in Boulder, Colorado, confirmed this to me. Since NOAA must now report on nongovernmental weather mod activity, Hess is in a position to know. He says this particular company is dead certain that seeding gives them an annual 10 percent hike in water volume for hydroelectric power and irrigation.

Weather modifiers like Irving Krick, Thomas Henderson, and Douglas Elliott are part of a small, hardy, adventurous band who want to blaze new trails in the sky, a bit like the flying "barnstormers" of the 1920s. Will their activities precede a revolution as world-encompassing as the machines that swim in the air? The answer is still ahead of us and is influenced somewhat by their sales ability.

The five or six best companies will do a properly controlled experiment before they start seeding, to be as sure as possible the conditions are propitious. But for most operators this procedure is too expensive, and the customers refuse to pay for it, so they go ahead without really knowing what the meteorological facts are and do their work in a shotgun fashion—just seeding whatever clouds their practiced eyes tell them will respond.

Lightning Control

In 1752 Benjamin Franklin and French physicist d'Alibard staged experiments, within one month of each other, to document their belief that thunderclouds were electrified.[2] They proved their point. For about 170 years after that no one learned much more about lightning. But in recent years scientists have explained that a thundercloud is a sort of electrostatic generator which produces electrical charges, both positive and negative, and then separates them so that each type becomes concentrated in different parts of the cloud. After a sufficient buildup, the positive and negative charges leap to rejoin each other, or other opposite charges on the ground. This "grounding" of the plus and minus ions resembles the way electricity jumps across the two points of an auto's spark plug. Lightning is simply a tremendous spark.

As lightning runs jaggedly through the sky it heats the air column around it, for a few microseconds, to about 54,000°F. This sudden momentary searing expands the air so explosively that it creates intense sound waves, which are heard as thunder.

Fig. 1. Lightning is simply a tremendous spark made when plus and minus ions in a storm cloud join each other, or opposite charges in the ground. (Photo by NOAA)

Lightning ravages trees, property, and man himself, and kindles forest fires. In the Apollo moon ship series, lightning also endangered the complicated electronic control mechanism at time of launch.

On moon shots and the Soyuz-Apollo hookup any storm clouds in the Florida area were considered a threat, and NOAA planes were readied to take countermeasures. For lightning these involved feeding the lower part of lightning-charged clouds with masses of metal chaff. They were intended to "ground" the gathering electric charges before they reached the strength that results in lightning. Tests verify that this device can actually decrease the voltage of lightning bolts.

I called up Michael Collins, veteran of the first man-on-the-moon trip, to see what he thinks about space flights and lightning. I found he recalls vividly what happened to Apollo 12 in 1969. Lightning hit the tip of the rocket shortly after it left the ground and ran right down the sides into the space capsule, where it messed up the entire communications system. "All the circuit breakers popped," Collins told me, speaking from the more peaceful atmosphere of his present office as director of the Air and Space Museum in Washington. The electronic devices, he said, "presented the crew with totally confusing and frightening information. Fortunately, the crew kept cool and didn't believe the signals that said the rocket was upset. They just rode it out and the temporary disruptions righted themselves. If they'd panicked they might have aborted the flight needlessly."

Collins said that until that incident none of them paid much attention to the threat of lightning, although they were watching all other weather factors. But after that, NASA was careful not to clear a flight while there was any hint of lightning in its path.

Although experiments with lightning control indicate some positive results, it is too soon to count on it for insulating manned space launches. But as the technique is perfected, we can at last step one notch ahead of the Franklin lightning rod, which is virtually all we've had until now.

Speaking of lightning, a sudden electric storm recently felled the colorful professional golfer, Lee Trevino, in the midst of a match; and he was hospitalized briefly. His respect for lightning has grown sharply; he's not likely to volunteer to fly into the clouds to stop it with metal chaff—or even a magic wand.

Hurricane Abatement

Since a full-fledged hurricane releases energy equaling more than 400 twenty-megaton bombs in one day, it seems foolhardy for any man to get in its way on purpose, much less try to curb it.

But the Weather Service has been getting in the way of hurricanes for years. They monitor the intensity and direction of each storm so as to warn the people in its path.

Meanwhile, NOAA has been bravely probing into how to "housebreak" these raging menaces. They have tried, for example, to calculate the effect of cloud seeding outside the eye of hurricanes. They have built up some solid evidence for the hypothesis that it is possible to widen a hurricane's eye, reduce the rate of speed at which pressure changes as the storm center approaches, and slow down the hurricane winds. NOAA's project to do all this is called "Stormfury." So far Congressional appropriations are too small to pursue the existing plans until 1978. But hurricanes over the United States usually cause half a billion dollars in damage annually, not counting the human toll in lives and pain.

For more than a dozen years now, NOAA's scientists have been hurling themselves at full-blown hurricanes in large planes like the four-jet C-130 Hercules of the United States Air Force. This is a huge workhorse airplane, usually used for transport of troops and munitions. There are only about nine hurricanes in the North Atlantic each year (seventy, worldwide) but the storms are so vast (anywhere from 250 to 500 miles in diameter) and so complicated that years of study may be necessary before we can understand them well enough to know to what extent they are controllable. But they are so destructive it behooves us not to delay our research. Hurricane Agnes, in 1972, killed 118 Americans and destroyed $3 billion worth of property. Every year the death and damage totals should impel the United States government to speed up programs like Stormfury—but they don't.

Dr. Noel LaSeur directs NOAA's hurricane research lab in Miami. He is responsible for the Stormfury project. A thoughtful and friendly man in his fifties, he hides the frustration he must suffer over lack of budget for his mission. Nevertheless, other studies are in process. In September of 1976 Dr. LaSeur invited me to ride a Hercules into the next hurricane that matured in the Caribbean. But there were no more hurricanes that season.

Meanwhile, talks with veterans enabled me to visualize a trip through these storms. Dr. Robert Simpson (known as "Mr. Hurricane" after a long stint as director of the Miami Hurricane Center), his wife, Dr. Joanne Simpson, and Dr. LaSeur describe them marvelously. However, I suspect them all of underplaying the peril involved. A World War II air hero currently president of an airline, Bruce G. Sundlun, assures me that anyone who purposely flies into a hurricane must be semiinsane. Yet Joanne Simpson, who has ridden many a hurricane, says it's really more comfortable than puncturing single cumulus clouds.

"I've come back green in the face from our cumulus trips, but had my cup of coffee sitting unspilled on the table with my notes in Stormfury flights."

"That's right," adds her husband, "and the reason is that although winds can blow up to two hundred miles per hour you don't notice it much in the plane because the acceleration is steady. Of course, if you fly into the eye, then there's a jolt, for the wind abruptly drops from the highest speed to a light breeze. There's a heavier jolt when you've crossed the center and hit the eye wall again on the opposite side—for you're leaving relative calm and entering the storm where the wind roars fastest. Bad turbulence comes when a hurricane makes a landfall and breaks apart. Then, instead of smoothly whirling air, you have it going every which way. The worst and wildest is when the eye traverses an island, particularly if there are hills on it."

"True," says his wife. "Once our people were tracking a Caribbean storm and the eye suddenly went over a mountainous island—as they were flying in the eye—and one of the crew was thrown so hard he broke his back."

Not since the French Curies worked together on radium has a family jointly gained such respect in science as the Simpsons.

As might be deduced from the familiarity of NOAA people with the hurricane, they have pretty well analyzed its basic formation and its fluctuations.

What exactly is a hurricane, or cyclone, or typhoon? (These, by the way, are different names for the same type of storm, depending on where it occurs. I use them interchangeably in this account.) Simply put, a hurricane is a cyclonic disturbance in the tropics, rotating about a low pressure center (the eye) moving at 5 to 50 miles per hour, with winds from 75 to usually not more than 150 miles per hour, and with profuse rain. It begins over the open sea, and usually splinters to its end over land.

To steer it or abate it we must know much more than we do; but we already know that it collects its enormous strength from four different natural engines:

First, when solar rays heat the ocean's surface sufficiently—to 79°F or more—it heats the air above, which then expands and rises. The rising air is humid with evaporated salt water, like steam from a boiling pot. Usually the ocean radiates solar heat safely back to the sky causing no fuss in the atmosphere. Only under certain, not clearly comprehended mixes of temperature, barometric pressure, winds, and evaporation will it start cooking up a cyclone.

Second, in the clouds some two to three miles above the sea, the temperature drops and precipitation simultaneously releases the latent heat of evaporation, which causes more convection, lifting the air still higher. The two combined drafts of hot air rush upwards faster. The air is "draining" upward as the water in a basin drains downward. It starts whirling counterclockwise in the northern hemisphere, clockwise in the southern.

A third engine kicks in when the air finally cools at about 17,000 feet: Gravity then pulls the air down toward the ocean, which warms it and moistens it; it becomes buoyant and once more soars, spinning toward the chill lid above. This process continues, like the action of a pump, until the cyclone passes over cooler water or land, thus cutting off the warm updraft. One way to interrupt a hurricane is to lay a thin, oily membrane on the sea surface at the foot of the eye. This would presumably stop the evaporation which feeds the storm.

A waterspout is a miniature version of this phenomenon, but lacks the pump mechanism and the rain which enlarge and complicate the structure of the hurricane. A waterspout lasts only a few minutes. The hurricane may last five days, during which—with modern weather reporting in the public news media—people living along the storm track can either shiver with apprehension, or plan thoroughly to avoid its oncoming wrath, or just ignore it entirely.

A fourth engine moves the burgeoning storm toward its destination: the general atmospheric movement in the area where the hurricane matures (only one in ten matures fully). The meandering route of this lateral movement defies accurate measurement or prediction. About all the forecasters can say is that when a storm pauses, it is about to change course.

The doughnut shape of a hurricane (four simultaneous hurricanes can be seen in the NASA photo, figure 2) is the ultimate product of these forces and phenomena. Satellite pictures cannot show us the actions of the four "wind engines" that produce the hurricane's fearful intensity. We can only see the clouds—their "exhausts." But we can also observe one phenomenon not mentioned in this intentionally simplified description: the numerous bands of rain, each of which keeps generating its own convections of air, which then cool and tumble back to the sea, only to rise again.

The central eye of the storm is the vortex through which the hot

Fig. 2. This NASA photo, August 29, 1976, catches the huge swirls of four simultaneous hurricanes—three in the North Atlantic, one in the Pacific off Baja California.

air pours upward. This flow causes a partial vacuum at sea level which draws in the cool air spilling from the top of the eye in the pump action already described; it also causes the great drop in barometric pressure at which even the bravest sea captains quaver. This lessens the weight of the atmosphere on the sea, so that the sea level rises; and the wind-driven waves pile up more water as the storm nears the coast. The combination produces what is known as "storm surge," an abnormal rise in sea level along the shore. The storm surge and the fierce, house-busting winds give the hurricane its one-two punch. Storm surges have raised the sea as much as twenty-five feet (as happpened during Hurricane Camille) for tens of miles of shoreline. The greatest storm tide of all (about forty feet) struck the mouth of the Hooghly River in India's Bay of Bengal in 1776.

Drenching rains add another punch. Hurricane Agnes dumped 25.5 cubic miles of rainwater that just about washed the northeastern United States into the Atlantic Ocean.

National Weather Service advisories have radically reduced human casualties from wind and storm surge. However, property damage keeps increasing because of the rapidly rising number of seashore cottages.

In poorer countries thousands may die as they did in Bangladesh, when a typhoon tore away countless sea-level shacks. Although the poverty-burdened people were aware of the onrushing menace, they lacked the means of transport to safe havens inland.

Peter Thacher, deputy head of United Nations Environment Program, wants to put out a brochure entitled "How Natural are Natural Disasters?" Thacher, an American friend of mine, grimly discussed this with me. He feels a booklet would be one step toward reducing the damage in "disasters" by giving instructions to help prevent havoc—at least in the poor, disadvantaged parts of the world. His point is that if people knew how to move away from imminent storms and were properly forewarned many would survive who would otherwise perish.

Meanwhile, NOAA planners continue to study the hypothesis that seeding hurricanes may somehow reduce their destructiveness by softening their peak intensity (which causes the worst of the wreckage)—that is, by expanding the area of the hurricane, thereby mitigating its impact at any one point.

There are three possible risks in controlling hurricanes (when and if we learn how to do it):

One risk is that to dismantle the hurricane in any way might also cut the amount of essential rainwater it carries to crops and animals and man.

Japanese officials are uneasy on this point, for they know that NOAA has been considering moving their hurricane study project, Stormfury, to the Far East. Some Japanese experts have remarked that Japan is "blessed" with typhoons and they would rather lose lives than soften the thrust of their beloved typhoons. They fear that a Japan deprived of typhoon water may undergo greater human harm than a few unfortunate victims of the storm. Nevertheless, if seeding really works, Japan would doubtless be happy to see typhoon destruction minimized as long as it is done without losing any rain.

Another risk is that man's meddling may redirect a hurricane onto a collision course with some populous city. To avoid this, NOAA's rule is to seed no hurricane nearer than fifty miles to the shore. Australia, still stung by the razing of Darwin by Cyclone Tracy in 1974, has established a tighter restriction (even though Tracy was *not* seeded): no experimenting with a cyclone that could reach land within twenty-four hours.

A third risk is that widening the hurricane might expand the lethal storm surge.

Despite these possible disadvantages I believe it is a shame not to support any scheme that might abate hurricanes.

One possibility we might try is to detonate explosives deep in the ocean under the hurricane's eye. This would supposedly replace warm surface water with cold water and thus deny the storm one of its sources of energy.

It seems likely that as scientists and engineers learn more about these mighty tempests they will conceive of new ways to curb them. The best score so far came from NOAA's Dr. Cecil Gentry's seeding of Hurricane Debbie (in 1969), which reportedly slowed its winds by 15 percent. Most scientists agree that this record is encouraging, though not conclusive. As in all weather modification, the trick is to separate natural fluctuations from those wrought by seeding. This is tough to do because hurricanes are in constant flux: you just can't find one that holds steady.

Robert Simpson argues that we should study typhoons that occur near the Philippine Republic: "There are some nineteen typhoons per year in that zone; hence with good luck we might be able to accomplish more in one year than we did in fifteen years in the United States, when we seeded only eight times in four storms."

Simpson's belief stems from noticing that airplanes flying through hurricanes collect rime on their wings. But, he admitted to me, these planes have flown through only a small fraction of the total number of storms, so we know only that this small fraction of the storms is wet and supercooled—the preconditions necessary for fruitful seeding.

The Japanese meteorologists are afraid that we also don't know whether the typhoon cloud structure contains enough moisture to respond to the seeding.

Despite our experiments, we don't really know how a hurricane will react to seeding. We can't make enough of the necessary assumptions. For example, we can't yet describe in any model how a single cumulus cloud behaves in a hurricane—and that's only one component of the hurricane, among dozens.

As Simpson concludes, "modeling must go hand in hand with open-air experimentation, with direct observation of the storm, the seeding, and the reactions to seeding".

To modify weather successfully, in other words, we need to be able to predict what it's going to do on its own. The trouble is we can't do that well enough yet. Simpson pleads that the way to break out of this impasse is to go ahead and make careful weather modification experiments to learn what we have to know—both for predicting weather and modifying it. This is not exactly a watertight bit of logic, but it gives sharp voice to the impatience of both weather predictors and would-be typhoon tamers.

When all this argumentation is boiled down it tells me, in simple logic, that given the incredible costliness of hurricanes there is no excuse for not pursuing every clue we have as to how to combat them.

Tornadoes (figure 3) occur in all parts of the world. Like a hurricane or waterspout, a tornado consists of hot air spinning upward from a sun-heated surface and following a route that is wobbly and unplottable, except that it starts and finishes over land, not water, and carries no rain in or around it. It is viciously violent and can hoist housetops, large animals, and even cars into the sky. It

Fig. 3. Tornadoes: No one can even theorize intelligently how to intercept or modify them. (Illustration by NOAA)

travels at 25 to 60 miles per hour with 500-mile winds; the sudden low pressure at the center can explode a barn or house. No modifier of its voracious vortex has get been devised.

Weather Modification Overseas

Weather modification has been studied or practiced in Kenya, South Africa, Niger, Switzerland, the USSR, Czechoslovakia, Israel, Thailand, Okinawa, Australia, China, Jamaica, and Brazil. There is a new demand for help in curing droughts in the United States and in some of the dawning nations. The United States Agency for International Development (AID) has handled overseas requests charily, stating that this is an uncertain science and AID will happily provide data and some technical advice, but no dollars and no official consultants.

As a result, a number of American "weather mod" personalities have responded as unofficial consultants. The Doctors Simpson, now at the University of Virginia; Merlin Williams of NOAA's Boulder, Colorado, office; and Pierre St. Amand of the United States Navy's China Lake, California, research lab have been well received abroad as weather fixers in the Philippine Republic, Niger, and Israel.

Always on the lookout for ways to balance its water deficit, Israel has jumped at this new opportunity and already boasts a notable record in rain production. Dr. Neuman, the Israeli project director, has improved existing techniques to such a point that he can affect a whole region with seeding.

Merlin Williams reports that on the edge of the Sahel Desert, he helped the government of Niger get a seeding program going in five days. The Sahel runs along the southern limit of the Sahara, from the Atlantic coast for about 3,000 kilometers. The seeding was followed by rain—right in the middle of the terrible recurring drought. The following year, Williams continues, Niger experts copied our procedures and had their first normal rainfall in eight years—again with his consultative assistance. It may be that seeding brought the rain. But there is after all no objective, independent study to confirm his success story.

At the invitation of the Philippine Republic, St. Amand completed extensive test seeding with the government officials. He has since set down the methods used and the findings of this collaboration in a detailed and convincing handbook on rainmaking. He is certainly the most enthusiastic and articulate proponent of this new "art." One or two of his peers in the profession deem him a bit too much of an advocate. I would say to them that St. Amand's personal dynamism is an asset in winning public and congressional support and dollars for research. Without the drive and confidence of men like St. Amand, weather modification could dry up and die in its infancy.

How does the cause of weather modification stand as of this writing? The overall chief of NOAA, Commerce Secretary Elliot Richardson, stated to me in 1976 that he considers weather modification extremely valuable. When you have the beginnings of a technology with so much potential, he declared, you should push hard to bring it to maturity.

Richardson's successor under President Carter, Mrs Juanita M. Kreps, is subject to the National Weather Modification Policy Act of 1976. This orders the secretary of commerce to develop a national policy.

This act may just be the best news for "weather mod" since Schaefer made snow in 1946. It calls for the secretary to report within one year on the state of scientific knowledge concerning weather modification, its technology, and its problems. The law spells out Congress's intent to have a "national program of weather modification research and development."

Vincent Schaefer and his colleagues in the Weather Modification Association (WMA) must be gratified with the new law. I attended the 1976 WMA annual meeting in Los Angeles and detected their unanimity on only one point: Commerical operators have gone as far as they can in weather control; now it is up to the government to step in and take the technology forward.

It was also apparent to me that WMA puts Vincent Schaefer on a pedestal. Like Charles A. Lindbergh, he is an individualist who "did it first," and others have built on his achievement.

For over two hours I questioned Dr. Schaefer. As we sat chatting on a park bench in the pale, smoggy sunlight of Los Angeles, I remembered my father interviewing Lindbergh before and after he soloed the Atlantic in 1927: This was in preparation for the flier's first book *We*,[3] of which my dad wrote a third.

"How can you afford the expense of so much high altitude research without backing?" I asked, knowing that Schaefer constantly studies air pollution particles in many countries, often at heights thousands of feet above sea level. His answer was characteristically homespun:

"Why, I take readings on mountaintops"—he is an ardent backpacker like his late mentor, Langmuir—"and inside scheduled airliners. I place my air quality sensor next to the ventilating duct that brings in air above each passenger's seat. I have been able to calibrate these values with those outside the plane and proved them accurate."

His replies to my many questions about the future boil down to his belief that the slowdown in weather modification is a "people problem," not a scientific one.

As I recall that day in 1976, I now realize that mere government initiative will not suffice to lift this new profession out of its doldrums. It will also take the Lindbergh or Schaefer brand of inspiring personal leadership.

3

SNOW, ICE, SEA, SKY, AND EARTH SURGERY TO IMPROVE THE WORLD

Heavy snow thudded against our faces driven by a twenty-five-knot wind with thirty-five-knot gusts, as it had been for nearly twenty hours. Despite the wind the snow wasn't drifting much. The flakes were too wet and thick and they lay in a new twelve-inch blanket that covered another foot of crust from an earlier storm. We shivered and huddled against each other like cattle for mutual warmth. We weren't saying much; the blizzard that looked so thrilling from our playroom had become our enemy. "Think of the poor Eskimos," we murmured to each other. "I wish Daddy was here," whimpered my seven-year-old sister." He'd build us an igloo!" "Shut up," we told her, we older ones—six of us, including cousins and neighbors. "You can't make igloos here. This is Wood-mere, Long Island, not Greenland." "If Daddy came he'd make an igloo—you'd see," she repeated a little more stridently.

We ignored her.

A few desultory attempts to make a snowman fizzled. Too cold. Too miserable. We turned on Cousin Jimmy and washed his face

57

with snow. Not much fun either. Snow got down everybody's neck. The gray light around us lessened. It was getting dark sooner than usual. "When can we go in the house?" someone whined. "Not for an hour," answered my brother. "Mother said we have to get some air!"

A deep, cheerful voice suddenly shattered our gloom.

"Hi, kids, enjoying yourselves?" A tall, ruddy-faced figure appeared, snow spilling off his brown fedora onto his gray tweed coat. Dad had come home early from his office in New York. He never did this.

"Make an igloo," said my sister, single-mindedly.

"Anyone else want an igloo?" asked Dad.

"Sure!" came an unbelieving chorus.

"Well, let's go!" shouted Dad. "First of all, you . . ."

It was a miracle. With a long bread knife he cut large blocks out of the snow and told us how to fit them together in a circle; then lay a second smaller set on them; then a third much smaller; and finally the last block—a white keystone—with a little air hole. In a jiffy Dad carved out a door at ground level and called for the family steamer rug and a candle. We all crawled inside and sat cross-legged and snug on the rug. Our bodies quickly heated the interior to a Florida temperature and the guttering candle became a wan tropical moon.

"Wait a second," said Dad, veteran of a four-year Arctic expedition. "We need a mug-up!" Minutes later we were eating hot apple sauce sandwiches. My sister, eyes sparkling, was silent at last.

Gone were the storm and our discomfort. In thirty minutes of fascinating, feverish activity we won our first battle in man's ancient war to improve his surroundings.

The rest of childhood was a kind of anticlimax, in terms of environmental modification. True, we kept building—towers, tree houses, and underground huts—but we never duplicated the thrill of creating warm, dry weather in the midst of a blinding blizzard.

In chapters 1 and 2 we saw what's in store as to controlling the weather through short-lived manipulation of clouds. Let's turn now to more long-lived control over significant moving parts of the planet—rivers, sea currents, polar ice sheets, the plates that shift during earthquakes, and the atmosphere.

Through thousands of years of cutting forests, planting crops, and even manicuring one-lot lawns, our species has fine-tuned the local environment without much concern as to how our local actions will affect the ecosystem.

On a broader scope, our dams, artificial lakes, irrigation systems, millions of miles of concrete roads, more millions of square miles of tarmac and cement airfields and parking lots and cities have given us what we want—or thought we wanted. Happiness, as one philosopher said, is not just getting what you want; it's wanting what you get. But one fact is clear: that our "improvements" have upset the ecological equilibrium established by nature during aeons and have thus netted us a net loss in the quality of our environment. Naturally in my six years with the Environmental Protection Agency I encountered countless examples of such losses, at home and abroad.

Take the Aswan Dam on the Nile. Upstream the dam backs up the river into a beautiful lake—called Lake Nasser—300 miles long and bountifully stocked with fish. Not very high-grade fish, actually. I saw them by the hundreds in Aswan—fat, flaky catfish lying in racks ready for shipment. The ice packed around them melted in the sunlight where they awaited trucks to carry them to market. I gagged inwardly at them; they looked barely edible. How would they taste, I wondered, after a long journey in the heat, with the ice gone, followed by another wait at the local store, and then being carried home clutched in a wrapping of wet, ink-smudged newspaper?

Downstream, the late President Gamal Abdel Nasser promised his countrymen, the dam would stem the annual floods, furnish more water for farms throughout the year, yield abundant hydroelectric power, and do much, much more.

The dam has honored the majority of Nasser's pledges, but allegedly it has added some ugly extras. First, the nutrient-rich silt which once gave sustenance to the soil along the riverbanks and to the once plentiful fisheries at the delta in the Mediterranean, is now trapped behind the dam in Lake Nasser; therefore, the farms along the river now require more fertilizer and the delta fisheries have dwindled to a few hungry sardines and herrings. Without the floods to flush out liver flukes, the terrible, debilitating disease bilharzia afflicts more sufferers every year. Evaporation from the expansive surface of Lake Nasser (inaccurately estimated by the planners) is enormous: The fierce tropical sun delivers heat like a tremendous blowtorch, and daily steals millions of gallons of the water that was destined to flow through Egypt. The lake itself won't fill for 200 years because of the evaporation and seepage around the base of the dam. Critics swear that all the above is true.

If so, I can't help thinking how time changes our ideas of what we thought were the mistakes of history. In 1956, Secretary of State John Foster Dulles reneged on a United States offer to help fund the dam. I was a diplomat in Israel that year and remember the tremendous reaction to Dulles's political miscalculation. Dulles informed the Egyptian ambassador of the decision rather disagreeably; and Nasser was so furious that he closed the Suez Canal to the West and quickly accepted a Soviet loan for the dam. Dulles took plenty of public abuse in the United States for this cold war faux pas which had driven Egypt into the arms of the Soviets. However, if the dam turns into an ecological ugly duckling, at least Dulles can be credited for making the right decision environmentally.

In any case, it's too soon to make final judgment, since the ecological research is incomplete at this writing. Egyptian scientists are collecting and examining evidence to get at the truth. Ironically the United States is aiding them with funds and technical assistance, provided by my office in EPA.

Dr. Mustafa Hafez of Egypt's national academy of science and technology told me in Cairo early in 1976 that the dam has "brought us no problems which we cannot solve." He is in a good spot to talk about the dam's effects, since he directs our five-year binational, study "The Ecological Impact of Impounding the Nile at Aswan." EPA is comanaging this million-dollar project. The money comes from American-owned Egyptian pounds which can be spent only in that country: The United States government acquired the pounds in payment for United States wheat sold to Egypt at bargain rates under the supervision of Secretary Dulles.

Despite the errors that ensue when civilization advances at the expense of its natural life-support systems, we keep cooking up ways to do nature one batter, on an ever more ambitious, sophisticated, and exotic scale. Some of these dreams will move smoothly into realization and will enrich us all, the poor as well as the powerful, with no hurt to the environment. Others may end abruptly in painful awakenings. Still others may prove to be no more than wild theories, like the theme of Jules Verne's *Purchase of the North Pole*, in which the protagonists try to jar the earth off its axis with a tremendous explosion so that the arctic will have a warmer climate.[1]

I will examine a number of fanciful hypotheses—some more practical than others—on how to rework the land, sea, and climate around us. These ideas won't necessarily please the reader. They may jar and worry him.

Orbit a Venetian Blind to Change the Climate?

I was lucky enough to talk with another renowned European-born genius. He outlined to me a more likely venture he's been thinking about, not for making money—it will take of lot of that—but for bending the climate to suit our wishes. This is native Hungarian Edward Teller, German-educated (University of Leipzig) as a physicist. Dr. Teller has been a naturalized American since 1941. Credited with creating the hydrogen bomb, he is still active in nuclear research.

Like Albert Einstein, Dr. Teller is so brainy in so many ways that others involve him in many pursuits. He is much sought after, for example, by the so-called "think tanks," where issues important to our nation's well-being are studied and debated. The Mitre Corporation is one, located in Virginia conveniently near the main offices of the federal government.

Knowing of my interest in new ways to control environment, the Mitre people generously asked me to a sandwich lunch with Dr. Teller at their headquarters. They figured that time spent with him would be valuable to me, since he believes peaceful nuclear explosions and other modern technology should be harnessed to face-lift the planet in various ways. His book *The Constructive Uses of Nuclear Explosives* spells out several, such as carving the earth with transcontinental canals and great reservoirs and harbors.[2]

My Mitre friends were right. As soon as the great man entered the simple office where we were to eat, he plunged into a description of one of his most grandiose concepts, after only the most perfunctory of introductions. Our three Mitre executive hosts sat quietly at the round table, obviously in some awe of Dr. Teller's brilliance. No one interrupted him for several minutes. I wondered if I would be able to understand him at all, much less enough to take notes.

He was elaborating on his theoretical design of a mechanism that might give man a steering wheel to control the climate of our globe. The idea is to place in space a few trillion tiny pieces of metal foil, much like the aluminum chaff which was used in World War II to deceive enemy radar. George Jacobs, formerly of the United States Information Agency, recalls how this worked one day when he was with the Eighth Air Force bombing the oil fields of Leipzig. The attacking planes were flying above a thick cloud cover but the antiaircraft guns were shooting at them accurately, guided by radar. "The flak was ferocious," Jacobs recounted to me, "but we were prepared with strips of aluminum chaff which when allowed to fall were supposed to look just like airplanes on the radar. So we dropped clusters of the stuff, and sure enough, the radar locked the guns right on to the chaff which, as it dropped, was still going at the speed of the planes. We veered away and completed our mission unhurt."

Teller was telling us that the foil he had in mind would physically intercept or reflect rays of the sun headed toward the earth. Dr. Teller went on to say that with this movable screen it should be possible to shade the tropics from excessive sunlight and give them a more temperate climate. This alteration would cut down the need for air conditioning, enliven workers, and widen the range of fruits and vegetables that can be raised there.

Dr. Teller answered my unasked question on how to get the foil to where it can steer the atmosphere into new weather patterns. "The shuttle," he began cryptically. Then I realized he meant the space shuttle that NASA (National Aeronautics and Space Agnecy) has been preparing for years, but which is not yet in operation.

"The shuttle should have a capacity of ten tons," Teller's booming rasp of a voice told us. "The cost would be close to a thousand billion dollars."

Dr. Teller spotted the flash of fiscal doubt in my eye, particularly in this time of ailing economies. Up to this point his demeanor had been firmly professional. Now his inside warmth and humor showed through: "You don't have to worry," he smiled. "I don't even know if it all will work. All I want right now is enough money to run a feasibility study. If the answer comes out positive then we can start to grapple with the big expenses. First we must learn what sort of reaction the foil shade over the earth will bring. If it turns out bad, we can vaporize it [out of existence] with laser beams."

Teller says the foil should be very thin, only a few thousandths of an inch. Also it can be made from various kinds of materials so that it can either absorb or reflect the sun's energy. "We can set it so that it will cast shadows over the equator and reflect solar heat toward the poles—simply redistribute the rays north and south. With this mechanism we should be able to make any kind of climate we want on earth."

A Russian, Professor M. I. Budyko, director of the Main Geophysical Laboratory, Leningrad, USSR, recently published a proposition for injecting a sort of chemical blanket into the atmosphere. Like Teller's orbiting metal foil, Budyko's blanket would reflect and thus redistribute the incoming solar heat toward the earth's northern areas. If this theory could be implemented, Canada, Alaska, Scandinavia, and China—along with the Soviet Union—would pick up a free bonanza of pleasant weather.

To form this reflective blanket, Budyko would inject quantities of sulfate aerosols—tiny droplets—into the stratosphere, *if* the present alleged trend to cooler temperatures continues. He would use sulfates because they are so easily available. The sulfur dioxide gas from auto and industrial emissions is present in clouds in the troposphere (the part of the atmosphere in which we live and fly our low-level airplanes) as are similar emissions from volcanoes and the ocean surface. We have learned from Scandinavia that acid rain and snow result from industrial pollution gas that converts naturally into sulfates. Sulfates would also be appropriate because they consist of such minuscule particles they will stay "in residence" (as the meteorologists say) in the stratosphere for long periods. Presumably Budyko envisions thrusting the sulfates into the stratosphere with the kind of rockets the Soviets employ for hail reduction operations.

Instead of a carton of silver iodide crystals to be exploded into the hail cloud, the sulfate package would burst at the height desired for his sulfate mirror (or blanket), which would then stay in place, maybe for years.

In 1976 the Soviet government asked Budyko to check out a report—possibly the CIA summary circulating that year—that a cooling trend was on the way which would bring lower crop yields in the Soviet Union resulting in insufficient food for the people.

"Give us your estimate of what is ahead for climate," is reportedly what the government asked Budyko and a colleague. They have already complied; and their opinion differs totally from that of the Americans: Because of rising levels of carbon dioxide in the atmosphere, we can look forward to a *warming* trend for the next decade or so. Their statement doesn't necessarily indicate a consensus in the Soviet Union, for there are at least a dozen or so top climatologists and we have heard from only two. It does suggest, however, that Budyko won't be recommending any climate correcting for the coming ten years.

Dam the Bering Strait to Improve the Climate?

To journey from Uelen, Siberia, to Tin City, Alaska, by boat entails a chilly fifty-six-mile ride across the Bering Strait. Fourteen thousand years ago, during the last major Ice Age, you could have walked across an isthmus that connected Asia and America. This was possible because the ice drew so much water out of the oceans that the sea level dropped 150 feet from what it is now; and the average low point of the Bering Strait is only about 120 feet above the present sea level; so the land bridge thus formed was 30 feet above the sea. Some blue-sky advisors have urged that the government construct an artificial causeway across the Bering Strait. In 1972, a Catholic University physics teacher named Clyde Cowen said, that if you dam the Bering Strait (as he explained it to Washington officialdom) you will bring some fine and fancy improvements to the climates of North America and Siberia.

This idea didn't originate with Cowen, nor maybe even with the Soviets, although it had appeared years earlier in their scientific journals. It is a theory that numerous geophysicists and climatologists have written and talked about lately. They believe that if you bottle up the chill Arctic sea instead of letting it flow south as it does now, then the northern Pacific will gradually warm up and the adjacent land masses will do the same. The temperature rise will put an end to present harsh winters so that additional crops will grow. People will be able to farm and live more comfortably than do the few hardy pioneer types who eke out a life in these frigid areas at present.

While this is a nice idea to toy with, avows Dr. Ronald

LaVoie, NOAA's deputy chief of weather modification, it's not one to count on—at least not yet. LaVoie is on record as saying that government policy is not to conduct an experiment of this kind unless we know what the eco-outcome will be. He said flatly that scientists are not able to prognosticate what would happen to the climate if such a dam were built.

There's another, more intriguing hypothesis (and it sounds more practicable) on how a Bering Strait dam might ameliorate the earth's northern climate. After building the dam, goes this theory, you'd pump water from the warm Kuroshio (Japan) Current over the dam into the Arctic Ocean. Energy harnessed from the moving current would provide the power for the pumping. After a while the ice sheet in the Arctic Ocean would start to melt. This process would be self-accelerating because, as the frozen white surface of the ice vanished into the dark sea, the albedo (reflectivity) of the areas affected would drop from around 60 percent to about 10 percent. In other words, instead of radiating back into the sky 60 percent of the incoming sun's rays, these areas would reflect only 10 percent. They would absorb the difference as heat; this would raise the water temperature, and melt the remaining ice faster.

At last, with all the ice pack gone, the albedo of the ocean would be much lower, more solar heat would be absorbed, and freezing would be unlikely to recur.

The end result would be that the greater heat in the Arctic Ocean would warm the air over the continents to the south and they would then enjoy a more moderate climate. Presumably, at this point, you could turn off the pumps in the Kuroshio Current.

With the present stampede of some scientists to tell the public that we're rapidly heading toward another Ice Age, it's comforting to imagine that maybe man can do something to stop it.

Certainly the two ideas just discussed need more study before we give them our confidence. Larry Booda, editor of the highly respected oceans magazine, *Sea Technology,* expressed his view in one word, "Hogwash!" As a former navy captain, Mr. Booda points out pragmatically that the Bering Sea is too shallow—particularly at the sill between the two continents—to transport any significant amount of water. Also, the Kuroshio Current is too far south to be used to warm the Chukelin Sea and Arctic Ocean on the north side of the Bering Strait.

It will take some elaborate research to test theorists and pragmatists against each other—to examine the question, for example, of possible floods if the Arctic climate eases to a point that would melt the Greenland ice cap. The average thickness of this ice cap is nearly two miles, over an area of close to a million square miles. The weight of the ice has depressed the land inside Greenland's coastal mountains to over a thousand feet below sea level. If the ice cap should thaw, ice water would flow into the surrounding sea and flood harbors and coastlines everywhere, to some extent. The global ocean would probably rise about twenty feet.

Melting the ice that floats in the Arctic Ocean would not raise sea levels any more than the melting of the "rocks" in a martini would cause the martini to spill over the top of the glass. In fact, since freezing expands water, the melting of the ice in a drink—or of the Arctic's floating ice field—would doubtless lower the fluid level a bit.

Blacken the Arctic Ice Pack to Ease the Climate?

The following scenario may be an impractical idea—but if cost is no object it can be carried out. The idea is to scatter a layer of a black powder (such as soot) on the polar ice pack, in order to lower its albedo. This will allow more solar warmth to penetrate the ice and melt it, and when the ice is gone the surface exposed to the sun will be that of the dark sea, with its lower albedo, which will be warmed by the sun and thus will eventually moderate the climate on the continents to the south.

The big drawback in this plan is the astronomical quantity of black dust that would be required to cover the whole frozen Arctic

Ocean. The cost would be out of practical sight at this time. But on all these out-of-sight geophysical "fix-its" we must remember that the last century has brought the electric light, telephone, radio, aviation, radar, nuclear explosives, television, high-speed computers, and men in space. What man can imagine he can very often realize.

Indeed, Alvin Toffler cries out that we have too great an ability to use our technological power to overcome obstacles. His book *Future Shock* says that this very ability has made nervous and spiritual wrecks of us. He worries not that we can't do anything we think of, but simply that neither we nor our environment will be able to absorb the fantastic advances we've made or are about to unveil. Perhaps environmental modification projects should be accompanied by "human impact statements" before they are given a go-ahead.

The Gulf Stream—a Sinister Influence on Climate?

The Gulf Stream carries heat, which it picks up in the tropical Caribbean, all the way up the Atlantic Coast of the United States and over toward the British Isles. Part of it becomes the Norway Current, which continues up past Norway and around to Murmansk. Finally, like a huge, lazy tongue probing the cavity in a sore tooth, it curls around Franz Josef Land and peters out in the vicinity of Spitzbergen. Not only do these thousands of miles of swirling warmth moderate the temperatures of western Europe, up to Scandinavia, and some of northern Russia, but they also may prove to be a key cause of the new Ice Age that is being predicted these days.

This theory was propounded by experts Ewing and Donn in *Science* magazine not long ago.[3] In brief, it holds that the warm Atlantic waters will increase the temperature of the Arctic Ocean progressively. This will stimulate great additional evaporation, which will probably be visible as "sea smoke" (towers of mist) reaching from the warm water into the cold arctic air above. This phenomenon will boost the humidity, leading in turn to greater precipitation, which at arctic latitudes will fall as snow. As the snow blankets the darker land, it will heighten the albedo, reflecting more of the solar rays. The snow cover will pile up and keep going further south, until glaciers grip more than half of North America. When this happens, the new Ice Age will have arrived. If this theory is valid, the only imaginable man-made remedy would be to try the scattering of black powder already described.

Earth-Moving to Bring Water?

As the planetary population zooms upward, we must find food for more mouths. To deliver a subsistence-level diet to the mass of people expected by the year 2,000—about seven billion, almost twice today's number—will require not only a commensurate increase in arable land, but land with a larger yield per acre. Present surveys agree that the great majority of the world's people are already underfed. Fisheries, which have provided a considerable proportion of the protein input, are diminishing steadily; the spate of oil tanker spills and overfishing by factory ships are contributing to the problem.

To increase the productivity of farms will call for additional fertilizer. This is available in part from the conversion of sewage sludge that gluts the perimeters of all large cities which have sewage treatment facilities. Once we develop a simple system for ridding the sludge of poisonous heavy metals (plus residual bacteria) it will serve well for the enrichment of farmland.

A far greater need will be for fresh water to allow millions of square miles of desert to be recycled into productive cultivation. Fortunately, the fertile minds of scientists are visualizing one solution to this problem for which the prognosis is more immediately promising than some of the ideas we've been investigating.

This one involves peaceful nuclear energy, known to bureaucrats as PNE. Dr. Teller's book *The Constructive Uses of Nuclear Explosives*[4] shows in detail how PNE can provide earth-moving capability at high speed, in high quantity, and at low cost. Digging by the use of explosives has been far more usual in the Soviet Union than in America. Teller and his coauthors tell of a channel nine miles long that was cut all at once in 1964 by the detonation of 9,352 tons of high explosives set in 1,936 holes from thirty to fifty feet deep—perhaps the world's largest simultaneous multiple explosion.

Single-minded environmentalists argue against PNE on the basis that any nuclear explosion generates radioactivity. Wilson Talley, Teller's principal coauthor of the book just mentioned (published in 1968) allies himself with the statement that "from all the information we can gather, dangers from radioactivity are not of a limiting nature in the constructive uses of nuclear explosives." This should be comforting, in light of Talley's assignment as EPA's research chief, with a team of nearly 2,000 under his direction and a budget of some $300 million annually to back up his views on pollution. Dr. Talley and I, being colleagues at EPA, discussed this point as lately as 1977, when he assured me that in PNE applications, radiation can be held to safe levels.

Reverse Rivers to Save River Water at the Risk of Worsening the Climate?

Peaceful nuclear energy will be a most desirable tool for reversing rivers, an idea for obtaining more fresh water that is now under study. If we wish, we can reverse the direction of a large river so that its salt-free, life-giving water will not drain uselessly into salty oceans.

But if we do that, we must be certain to send the river water to places it can be exploited usefully. The Colorado River was diverted by a storm about fifty years ago, and for several years it flowed into a deep natural sump at subsea level (−235 feet) in southern California. Before Bureau of Reclamation engineers rechanneled the Colorado back toward Mexico and the Gulf of Lower California some years later, the sump had metamorphosed into a lake 300 miles square which was appropriately named the Salton Sea. Salt in the soil, coupled with heavy evaporation in the blazing desert sunlight and the termination of inflow from the Colorado, are causing the Salton Sea to be more like the Great Salt Lake every day.

Yet along its shores flourish the lush fields of the Imperial Valley. Water from the Colorado, (delivered by the Coachella Canal, which stretches some seventy miles into the valley) sustains the valuable crops of oranges, lemons, and lettuce. Across the border the Mexican farmers grimace as they tend their alfalfa, the best they can do with the poorer quality Colorado water that spills into Mexico at Morelos Dam.

Return flows from the extensive Welton-Mohawk irrigation system near Yuma, Arizona, leach minerals from the soil; and these pour back into the Colorado just before it enters Mexico. The anger of Mexican farmers at this inequity, as they see it, was translated into political action by former President Luis Echeverría, who expressed dissatisfaction in Washington.

A presidential task force headed by farmer Attorney General Herbert Brownell, on which I represented EPA, took more than a year to figure out how to deal with the Mexican complaint. In September 1975 Mexico accepted our offer to improve irrigation methods at Welton-Mohawk and erect a desalination plant. As these promises are implemented, the farmers around Mexicali will soon have water as pure as that of their American neighbors in the Imperial Valley.

These arrangements have burdened us with trouble and expense. The desalter will cost several millions to install and operate, and will leave noisome brine which causes a pollution disposal problem for the United States. Lengthy arguments among the federal departments and the riparian states along the Colorado had to be heard before our task force could develop an American position for the talks with Mexico.

During all this effort I couldn't help secretly cursing our earlier action in rerouting the Colorado. If only we had let nature alone, there would have been no dirty Colorado water to argue about with Mexico, we wouldn't have had to build the Coachella Canal (since the Colorado was already running through the Imperial Valley), and maybe the Salton Sea wouldn't have become a dead sea but would have been an additional source of water for parched Los Angeles County and its environs.

I am not advocating that we now redirect the Colorado to the Salton Sea. That opportunity passed us by in 1941, when we locked ourselves into an agreement to let Mexico have at least a million and a half acre feet every year of what's left over from our own myriad uses of the river. When we signed the agreement, many times that volume of water was gushing across the border; now the river resembles a sluggish sow with too many piglets tapping her teats. There are so many demands for irrigation and drinking water on the United States side that we can barely accommodate the Mexicans with the amount specified in our agreement.

The Soviets have no such aggravation with the Pechora River. So their plan to reverse it will probably go ahead. As does the Colorado, the Pechora rises high in a great mountain range (the Urals), and there the similarity ends. The Pechora slides out of the mountains heading north and, losing little volume to the requirements of civilization, empties thousands of cubic feet per second of clean water into the Barents Sea in the Arctic. The Soviets need this fresh water in the south. They have figured out a conceptually simple method of getting it there: use nuclear explosives to dig a hundred-mile conduit through the mountains to the Kama River, which joins the Volga River network that eventually empties into the Caspian Sea.

Extensive irrigation has bled the Volga down to a relative trickle into the Caspian. Deprived of the former great Volga input, the Caspian has begun to dry up. The Pechora-Kama hookup would save the Caspian and still allow enough water for the Volga irrigation needs, plus all the demands for fresh water made on the Caspian by the cities and farms that ring its shores.

If one set of ecological zealots is nervous about employing nuclear explosives for such purposes, another group is positively frantic over the environmental impact of reversing the Pechora River. They point out that the Pechora presently puts vast quantities of sweet water into the Barents, thus diluting its salt content. If this dilution stops, say various scientists, the proportion of salinity in the Barents will be augmented to the point at which it will no longer freeze in the winter. If this happens, there may be a climatological domino effect, with incalculable results to other regions and countries. At this writing the Soviet government appears unperturbed by the allegations that it may be about to disrupt the environment and is going ahead with its plans.

The Dome Petroleum Company of Canada won official permission to do offshore drilling for oil in the Beaufort Sea in 1976. We in EPA raised these questions: What will happen if there is a blowout of an oil well? What eco-consequences will reach the Alaskan shores of the Beaufort? The answers were voluminous, for the Canadian environmentalists had completed over forty separate studies of expected effects on the polar ecosystem.

This is the kind of detailed scientific forecast that has not yet been done, to determine the climatic aftereffects of reversing the Pechora. Nevertheless, the American scientists I've interviewed think no harm will come, unless the switch in sweetness of the Barents Sea sets off some chain reaction unforeseeable with our present state of knowledge. I have discovered in years of collaborating with scientists that they can straddle an issue even faster than politicians.

Meanwhile, the Russians have been busily massaging public attitudes on the Pechora project. Izvestia announced from Moscow in June 1976 that the American scientist R. Neys said that "diverting rivers from north to south can bring about a change in angular velocity of the earth's rotation, which in its turn will lead to a change in the climate." Shades of Jules Verne and reclimatizing the North Pole! Izvestia went on to cite the opinions of its own specialists to the contrary. Izvestia also disputed the fear of some that withdrawing the flow of rivers now adding their warmth to the seas that border northern USSR will worsen the climate on an already cheerless coast. I have no information on that point except that people who have been there say the excruciating cold and dreariness of those shores can't be any worse.

The Soviets have studied the possibility that removing the warm flow will cause faster freezing in the Barents, and they believe that this tendency *will* dominate over the tendency of an increase in the sea's salinity to decrease freezing. In short, the average water temperature might be slightly lowered by the diversion of the Pechora waters. Therefore, it would seem the climate will not be likely to change, at least because of the absence of one river's effluent.

But the Soviets are reportedly weighing the pluses and minuses of sending other rivers away from the Arctic Ocean area: The Yenisey and Ov, for instance, have been mentioned for replenishment of water for farms in the arid regions near the Aral Sea (just west of the Caspian).

Perhaps anticipating domestic objections to moving around more rivers, Izvestia again pointed a finger at the United States, "revealing" that "Americans themselves are preparing to direct part of the flow of the Yukon, Fraser, Peace, and other rivers into enormous reservoirs in the Rocky Mountains."

I haven't been able to verify that rumor. But I did sit down with Dr. Teller and peruse a map of North America to see if it might make sense to reroute the Mackenzie River in Canada south to the thirsty western desert of the United States. We agreed it might work even better to lead the Saskatchewan to the Snake River, if the Canadians would accept the idea. Surely there must be some combination of diversions whereby the largely underemployed waters of northern North America can be moved south, where they might convert our deserts into a copious breadbasket. Our new president, Jimmy Carter, has said he wants to accomplish things that have never been attempted before. This could be one such project, with benefits to the United States and Canada. There might even be enough to share some of the water with Mexico.

If we and the Canadians did launch such an ambitious venture, however, we could anticipate the same outcries from ecologists, climatologists, and others that the Soviets are now hearing.

The Soviets have grown sensitive on this point, according to an American physicist I know who just returned from the USSR. Believing in good faith that he was there on the basis of an open information exchange, he said he dictated on tape each night at the hotel in Moscow what scientific knowledge his counterparts had given him during the day. When his secretary typed them up back home, she found, like Nixon's secretary Rosemary Woods, an eighteen-minute gap—the eighteen minutes concerning the Pechora diversion plan.

There's a more straightforward way to get moisture to the United States deserts, or any rain-robbed lands that lie in the lee of mountains: Blast a canyon through the range with nuclear explosives; then the wet air that has been blocked can flow through to the desert beyond. The expectation is that the wet air would yield precipitation even if it required a bit of cloud seeding. But I doubt the environmentalists would hold still for wrecking that much of the landscape. They've already lined up to obstruct development of shale oil and strip mining for coal. The radiation from so much nuclear blasting would surely inspire another stop sign, probably by EPA.

New Millstreams, Flowing Down from the Mediterranean?

In their northern desert the Egyptians have heen talking of glamorous plastic surgery on the face of nature. It involves the Qattara Depression, which is a sunken area northwest of Cairo, some thirty miles south of the Mediterranean and 450 feet below its surface. This pockmark in the desert measures about a hundred by thirty-five miles.

The Egyptians want to cut a ditch from the Mediterranean, line it with concrete, and let the sea drain into the Depression. The water coursing into the hole could turn hydroelectric turbines. These would furnish power, which could be used to operate a desalination plant. Thus the briny Mediterranean water could be sweetened for use on farms in the desert. It would be possible to regulate the rate of flow so that evaporation in the Depression would equal the amount of incoming water. This way the Depression would never fill up and the hydroelectric machinery could run forever—theoretically.

The Egyptians have not yet estimated what ecological spillover this fanciful engineering would bring, particularly in view of the wish to dig the canal with nuclear explosives. The Egyptian government has gently put a bug in the ear of the United States, hoping for technical and material assistance. So far the Americans have not taken any stand. With suspiciousness among neighbors still a fact of life in the Middle East, the United States would doubtless draw political flak for providing Egypt such great capability in explosives, even for a peaceful goal.

One approach would allow us to contribute to the Qattara development: to offer similar cooperation to Israel and Jordan. A conduit could run water from the Mediterranean to the Dead Sea. Mediterranean water could spin hydroelectric rotors, just as at Qattara, after nuclear explosives have chopped a canal into the Dead Sea. As at Qattara, the amount of cool water singing its way downward to the lowest point on the earth's surface $(-1,292$ feet) would be regulated so that it would evaporate in the Dead Sea as fast as it came in. The project would give Israel and Jordan hydroelectric power for as long as they wanted it—and were willing to maintain the artificial conduit and the giant paddles of the power plant. Voltage generated could run desalting machinery to convert vast quantities of the Mediterranean waters for use by farms in both countries.

If environmental statements should reveal that the radioactivity from nuclear explosives for Qattara and the Mediterranean-to-Dead-Sea canal would endanger the populations of Egypt, Israel, Jordan, and perhaps other places, there would always be a good alternative: modern mechanical equipment. What was good enough for Panama and Suez should suffice for Qattara and the Dead Sea canal. There is still plenty of Middle East oil left to drive modern machines far more efficient than the steam shovels that wrought the wonders of the world nearly a century ago.

Such a project has so far reached only the stage of informal discussions among politicians and engineers in Israel, with an over-the-shoulder glance at American aid possibility.

Earthquake Control? How's that Again?

In college we concocted a cocktail consisting of one third each of gin, rum, and bourbon. We called it the Earthquake, because if an earthquake should come along after you'd imbibed, you wouldn't notice it. That was about as close as anyone ever got to controlling an earthquake, until, during the early sixties in Colorado, the United States Army accidentally lent a helpful hand.

The army for years had been injecting liquid wastes deep into the earth near Denver, strictly to dispose of them. One day United States Geological Survey employees noticed that seismic incidents in the area were multiplying in number and frequency. They guessed that the army's disposal activities might be the cause. Sure enough, they observed that when the pumping slowed or stopped, earth tremors lessened commensurately in frequency and quantity; if the pumping recommenced, the rather small quakes began once more.

When analyzed, this sequence revealed that by serendipity the army had constructed a sort of seismic rheostat that would function where a fluid under pressure was jammed into the crevices and cracks around a fault line. The Geological Survey people wanted to play with this ready-made research toy, but were afraid to risk inadvertently unleashing a high Richter-scale quake so close to a big city.

They found a safer substitute in the oil field at Rangely, Colorado. There, the owners were filling a formerly used well with pressurized water in order to scavenge any remaining petroleum. Since all this was taking place under a geologic fault, the researchers had perfect laboratory conditions in which to pursue their new findings.

What was happening, they reasoned, was that the pressurized liquid was operating like a lubricant in a large engine. Take your car, for instance: Its oil pump forces refined petroleum into the tiny spaces between moving parts, which otherwise would not turn.

Similarly, the opposite sides of a fault, or split in the earth's crust, are sometimes pushed from underneath by the constantly mobile, hot, molten core of the earth called magma. Normally the sides of the fault don't respond to the subterranean push right away, because of friction from the roughness of the mating surfaces. If you could stand like a giant above the fault and squirt oil from a jumbo-sized oil can into the crack, the sides of the fault could slip by one another more easily. Any fluid along the fault line apparently provides such lubrication; and the result is that the two sides of the crack move sooner and more gently. Without the lubrication the fault (under pressure from the magma) is like a stuck door with a man pushing harder and harder to open it: When he finally overcomes the friction and the door flies open, woe to anyone standing just beyond it. By the same token, woe to any building or human that is standing above a miles-long fault line when one side of it finally jumps into motion in response to subterranean forces. We have seen what happens to cities, in photos of San Francisco, Tokyo, Managua, and others. What happens to people is recorded in the tally (table 1) recently published by *Time* magazine (we don't yet have the statistics of the 1976 China quake):

Table 1: HISTORY'S GREAT QUAKES

Year	Locale	Death Toll
856	Corinth, Greece	45,000
1556	Shensi, China	830,000
1737	Calcutta	300,000
1755	Lisbon	60,000
1883	Dutch Indies	36,000
1902	Martinique	40,000
1906	San Francisco	700
1920	Kansu, China	180,000
1923	Tokyo	143,000
1960	Agadir, Morocco	12,000
1964	Alaska	114[*]
1970	Peru	67,000
1972	Managua, Nicaragua	10,000
1975	Mukden, China	—[**]

[*] Although the loss of life was relatively small, this quake was one of the strongest ever measured, with a magnitude of more than 8.4 on the Richter scale.
[**] Unreported, but believed to be high.

So it is good news that the experiment at Rangely demonstrated the feasibility of earthquake control. We know at least that earthquakes can be manipulated whenever we can regulate the fluid pressure in a fault zone.

One fail-safe method suggested for avoiding hurt by earthquakes is to avoid them—get out of the area when they are predicted. Historically, however, quakes have arrived without warning or polite introduction. Only during this century have seismic monitoring stations been able to make any estimates at all as to when a quake is due. They share data on recorded tremors in one area and pass them along to other stations known to be on the same fault configuration. But this is still very imprecise as a method of quake prediction, and so far hasn't earned much credibility.

One positive product of the current United States-USSR environmental agreement has been five good years spent verifying the

Soviet methods of monitoring and forecasting earthquakes, which may be superior to our own.

As this is written a Mr. Henry Minturn has gained a moment of prominence in California for giving advance warning of a large tremor there; but his accomplishment has not received scientific validation. Quake-casting in the United States remains a sometime proposition.

The now accepted science of "plate tectonics" may evolve into a system of reporting and prediction that will be as useful as the present short-term forecasts. Certainly these can help our planning, all the way from an outdoor picnic to routing ships when we expect a hurricane. The plate tectonics concept was proven by six years of widespread deep-sea drilling by the *Glomar Challenger*, a strange-looking experimental ship.

Plate tectonics is the idea that the surface of the earth is divided into separate, semirigid but moving plates above the molten magma beneath. In a way they resemble the sliding, turning panels on the "endless belt" that delivers your baggage at modern airports.

Crust is constantly being formed anew from magma pressing upwards along the ocean ridges (figure 4). The plates, which are made of this crust, move away from each other at the ridges and meet at their opposite edges, where either they collide to bunch up into mountains, or one slides under another the way a deck of cards gets shuffled. The places where the sliding under occurs are called "subduction zones." The places where the tectonic plates meet or break away from one another is where quake action occurs.

One day we may be able to establish a remote control monitoring mechanism all along the cracks that separate the plates. The mechanism could be kept at the ready at all times, the way an oiler on a ship keeps walking around the engine room and lubricates the bearings at the first sign of trouble. At the first seismic "squeak" these devices could automatically activate the emergency button to release preset injections of fluid into cracks along a fault line that

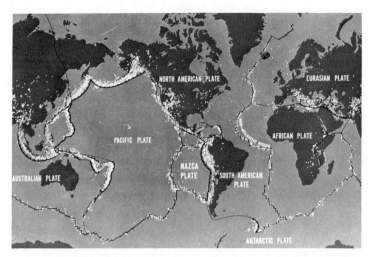

Fig. 4. Map of earth's plate structure. At subduction zones (heavy dark curves) such as the deep trenches ringing the Pacific, the leading edges of the plates plunge downward to be consumed in the mantle. Along the mid-ocean ridges the mantle wells up and solidifies as the ocean floor spreads. Plates run edge to edge along transform faults (thin curved lines). Dots mark earthquakes recorded in the last twenty years. (Illustration from the June 1976 report to the Federal Council for Science and Technology by the Ad Hoc Committee on Geodynamics)

is about to slip, thus reducing to a gentle lullaby a motion that might have been cataclysmic.

Miscellaneous Surgery

These are the large-scale operations which man, the geophysical surgeon, may one day perform on the not always patient patient, Earth. In the Patent Office we might find smaller-scale applications such as the ice dam designed by Athelstan Spilhaus—inventor, meteorologist, oceanographer, and writer. He says we could build dams of ice instead of earth and rock, so that when the lake they form gets silted up you could simply melt the dam. Then you'd freeze another dam above the silt pile. The silt pile, I suppose, could be carted away as fertilizer. The big refrigerators necessary to freeze the dam and keep it hard will be powered by hydroelectric generators on the site.

Such inventions keep popping forth. I remember one stranger who walked into my office in the United States Senate and said he could flush out the nation's major polluted rivers. His sketches showed that New York's Hudson River would be an appropriate one to begin with, because it has so much dirty water. You erect two dams, he was proposing, one at the Narrows and the other between the east end of Long Island and the Connecticut shore. You build them a few feet above the mean high-tide mark and let the river water rise to spillways at that elevation. Then the incoming tides, instead of pushing the garbage, sewage, and other filthy runoffs back upstream, simply pour them over the dams and into that great disposer, the Atlantic Ocean. The disadvantages of that scheme are so numerous I'll leave them to the reader to deal with.

Just as medical surgeons are always conjuring up new procedures to correct the physiological inadequacies of man, so man's desire to do the same with the globe we live on may be limitless. His ability along these lines is growing day by day.

We average citizens depend heavily on our Congress and executive branch to discard whichever of the new ideas are crackpot and choose those which can help to produce a more perfect world; but in a democracy it's ultimately the people who must serve as the watchdog: The public must be alert to new schemes and to their possibly unacceptable side effects. Thalidomide presumably served a useful purpose in medicine, but the birth defects that followed its use were horrible.

The tall tale of the too-tall woman is relevant. She persuaded a doctor to take seven-inch sections out of each leg so her height would be more normal for a woman. The surgery was successful but then she had a new complaint: "Doctor, my hands drag on the ground!"

The possible aftermath of the geophysical surgery now being proposed is not so easy to foresee. The furor in the Soviet Union over a new riverbed for the Pechora is a good thing. We should watch it carefully before reworking the rivers of our own continent. The environmental clamor over building the Alaska pipeline resulted in a much safer job's being done. Too bad analytic experts didn't get an early look at the plans for the Teton Dam, which later collapsed, or the Aswan Dam, which may turn out to be a disaster even more dire.

4

INSTANT GOOD WEATHER

The Franklin stove is one of the oldest tools for providing instant good weather that has been enjoyed by our society—and the bedroom air-conditioning unit one of the newest. The 1920s were a key decade in the history of such devices. The 1920s were a still-primitive era in many respects. Not many years had passed since the White House installed its first indoor bathroom (in 1851), and the announcement of it was met with derision and with complaints at the needless luxury being given to the first family!

At the beginning of the 1920s airplane pilots still sat air-blasted in open cockpits, and drivers of automobiles (which had windshields but no tops) had to spit out the dust and rain that blew in their faces, as people shouted from their piazzas: "Get a horse!"

Soon the airplane pilots had enclosed cabins; and by the late 1920s those motorists who wanted to could discard goggles and dusters and step into the prototype of the modern closed car.

In our houses steam radiators became more efficient; and with fuel cheap, Americans lived in overheated rooms. Hot-air registers were an improvement. Then the newborn insulation industry persuaded people to buy copper weather stripping to cut down drafts and colds. Ventilation had improved from the table electric fan and from the slow-spinning paddle on the ceiling in southern houses, to the attic fan from Texas—one which cools the whole house by drawing air through the cracks in doors and windows (even in insulated houses) and pumping it out through the roof. It's still the most efficient way to cool a house—and the cheapest. In 1927 the Holland Tunnel was completed, ventilated by gigantic fans at the entrances. According to the press release of the New York Port Authority, the environment down below was idyllic, with "fresh sea breezes" blowing through. In the thirties motion picture theaters began to offer crude air conditioning in the summer and their advertising posters carried paintings of winter scenes with snow and icicles.

The trend to ever more air conditioning reached its disagreeable zenith in recent years when architects designed office buildings with windows that won't open. The control of the air through central heating and cooling is supposedly less costly to operate when the system is not interrupted by letting in fresh air of any temperature.

The focus of this chapter is on artificial, man-made, or induced weather of a desirable kind. We've touched already on the thrill of the instant good weather humans attain by climbing into a fire-warmed cave, a body-heated igloo or hut, or an oil-, gas-, electric-, or sun-warmed or -chilled family dwelling of the present age. Now we will look at more remarkable examples of how to create the desired warmth or "coolth" or coziness in settings other than home and hearth. The imagination of modern man the environment maker is far more extraordinary than that of Omar the Tentmaker.

Writers and thinkers saw this coming generations ago and were troubled. Jules Verne, in *Twenty Thousand Leagues Under the Sea*, fashioned the fabulous Nautilus, which had music and fresh air and growing things—all in a submarine, which came to a bad end.

E. M. Forster in "The Machine Stops," written before 1914, saw it all in advance: the time in the future when civilization will have replaced nature; indeed, will have driven it out completely and put all habitation below ground. The characters each live in

> a small room, hexagonal in shape, like the cell of a bee. It is lighted neither by window nor by lamp, yet it is filled with a soft radiance. There are no apertures for ventilation, yet the air is fresh. There are no musical instruments and yet . . . this room is throbbing with melodious sounds.[1]

He saw the cold, personalitylessness of canned "Muzak" fifty years ahead of time, and told of

> those funny old days, when men went for a change of air instead of changing the air in their rooms![2]

The story is a parody on modern technology or "The Machine" at its stage of development sixty years ago. In the language of his yarn, Forster was sneering at the cult of living by The Machine. Forster's prophetic words when "The Machine" starts to disintegrate might be pondered today as we pound inexorably ahead toward an ever more artificial environment:

> and they knew (as they died) what had been important on the earth. Man, the flower of all flesh, the noblest of all creatures visible, man who had once made God in his image, and had mirrored his strength on the constellation, beautiful, naked man was dying, strangled in the garments that he had woven.[3]

This passage came to me sometimes at my office in the Environmental *Protection* Agency. There is a western exposure; and in the summer when Washington's afternoon solar fireball splashes in, the air conditioning stops and the heat snaps on, just as on winter mornings the heat snaps off and the air conditioning functions flawlessly.

It's curious how life's repetitions chase us. In 1953 I came to Washington rather than accept a job in the Lever Brothers Building on Park Avenue in New York City. The salary was inviting. The building was, and still is, the very pinnacle of lovely, modern glass design but the windows didn't open and still don't. This kind of building has prospered. But why live like a mole, in the sunshine?

Man Goes to Ground

Under certain exigencies our fellow being has managed to dwell underground handsomely, like mole royalty, you might say— under military exigencies. The Nazis, having invited the wrath of thousands of Allied bombers, burrowed to safety under the sod, where they located their most vital factories and some emergency medical facilities. If they'd had time and wherewithal they might have submerged themselves completely and escaped the whirlwind they reaped. Across the English Channel the doughty hero of empire wrote his speeches and planned grand strategy in a bomb shelter fit for a king's minister. Yet the shallower shelters were inadequate to give safe cover to the ordinary citizens on either side of the Channel.

Going underground is fantasy that intrigues us. W. F. Buckley, Jr., has sport with it in his book *Saving the Queen;* the hero says fliply to his gullible dinner partner at the White House:

> Operation Down Under. . . . All the President has to do is push one button and . . . the city of Washington sinks down five hundred feet and a concrete dome envelops us.[4]

Despite the relative peace of these times, the science of living underground is alive and well liked in several parts of the world. I have found myself comfortable and safe in the bomb cellar of the

Dan Hotel in Tel Aviv, well below sea level, during an air alert of the 1956 War. The North Vietnamese survived our B-52 strikes in elaborate mud tunnels. Under President Kennedy this country took a sudden crash course in building shelters under the guidance of a peace-loving Assistant Secretary of Defense, Steuart L. Pittman.

Pittman's civil defense plan designated caves and salt mines for housing up to 30 million refugees and incorporated a great deal of research on how to live in such conditions without being depressed. Pittman also persuaded local authorities to build schools underground that could be used by all citizens in case of nuclear attack. There are a number of arguments for operating schools beneath the earth's surface: There is less window-glass area to attract vandals; it is quieter underground and therefore easier for students to concentrate; and it is cheaper to heat or cool the schoolrooms, since the soil serves as natural insulation. In the years since Kennedy, this idea has caught on in Texas and New Mexico, where several below-surface schools save enormously on air conditioning. The ground where the building normally would be is free for athletics. The latest such school has just been completed in Reston, Virginia, primarily as a hedge against the energy shortage.

Meanwhile, the Pentagon's civil defense people are keeping an eye on the places we can dive into when (or if) a nuclear exchange occurs. Researcher George Sisson has turned up details about abandoned mines in Pennsylvania where 500 agriculturists are raising mushrooms. In—or rather below—Kansas City, Missouri, the Brunson Instrument Company has cut out 140,000 square feet of solid limestone for a place to locate its factory. In 1961, when civil defense became an issue (because of deteriorating relations with the USSR), a Mr. I. N. Stroud wrote an imaginative memo on "Subterranea."[5] This set forth a plan for reducing a city to a solid, underground cube, four thousand feet on a side. The advantage is that inhabitants can go just about anywhere on foot, or on endless-belt people movers. Since with this scheme there would be no polluting highways or smoky buildings on the surface, the whole area could be useful for out-of-door sports, hiking, camping, and related activity.

Three other Defense Department enterprises are delivering a constant stream of data on how to exist though buried. One of these is the standard Polaris submarine patrol, in which large crews of men stay submerged for three months at a time. Movies, study programs, hard work, fresh-frozen sirloin steaks, physical exercise regimes, and sunlamps produce healthy, contented veterans of these sunless cruises.

Sunk deep at Omaha, Nebraska, is another teeming military complex—the Strategic Air Command's (SAC's) headquarters. Security classification precludes my giving details, but fellow students of mine at the War College spoke of living and working in the depths of SAC for weeks at a time, if necessary. Never knowing what the weather is or whether the sun is shining gives the denizens of these artificial environments an eerie feeling which they all talk about at length.

Just as eerie is the day-to-day routine of our military scientists, engineers, and fighting personnel who are stationed at bases in Thule, Greenland, and at McMurdo Sound in the Antarctic. They stay in the extensive tunnels and caverns hollowed out in the permanent ice of those regions. If E. M. Forster could be resurrected and given a few weeks in one of these skillfully run, comfortably furnished, hidden habitats, I wager he would rewrite "The Machine Stops" with a happier finale.

One can only surmise how much further the present minor trend to underground building will continue. If even one nuclear device explodes in anger, there may be pressure to hasten the trend. If so the experimentation now going on will give us valuable guidance.

One result may be some fast study of the deep South Africa diamond mines, of Hitler's life in bunkers under Berlin, and of military duty in the inner recesses of the Rock of Gibraltar, where its defenders can disappear for months at a time. Or the final refuge of General MacArthur's soldiers on Corregidor Island at the mouth of Manila Bay; they were holed up in Malinta Tunnel. As a bomb disposal officer I inspected this tunnel after it had been wrecked with demolition charges. It was a high-vaulted, sizeable stone hideaway, with long barracks and hospital rooms leading off the central chamber—a tiny, capsule city. In case of a nuclear attack, we may need all the clues we can find on how to shoehorn target-area civilians quickly into the earth's crevices, natural or artificial. Because of the crumbling of disarmament talks with the Soviets, the United States House of Representatives has at this writing just voted a 50 percent increase in civil defense spending, so the topic is once again important in this country.

Meanwhile, underground living and working (or hiding) spaces are multiplying abroad, particularly in Sweden, in Switzerland (where the just-completed Sonnenberg Superhighway Tunnel through the Alps can double as perhaps the world's largest air-raid shelter), and in China, where the late Chou En-lai said that most of the cities were underlaced with networks of tunnels for safety should the "nukes" start dropping.

All this scurrying below doesn't take us too far from *Walden*, in which Henry David Thoreau said

> I dug my cellar . . . where a woodchuck had formerly dug his burrow . . . I took particular pleasure in this breaking of ground, for in almost all latitudes men dig into the earth for an equable temperature.[6]

How to be Cozy Beneath the Waves

Off Saint Croix in the Virgin Islands the tourist department has established the first underwater park. It lies next to small Buck Island and a trail for gawking scuba-ites is marked with signs about fifteen to twenty feet beneath the surface of the bay. This could be one vacation activity for the undersea hotel envisioned by some inventive engineers. "Subhotel" could be located anywhere on a continental shelf. Each room would feature a large porthole. In sites deeper than 150 feet, the building would have floodlights playing through the surrounding water twenty-four hours a day. Kelp "trees," coral, and other underseascaping could be arranged artistically to provide a view. The lights would attract all kinds of fish. Barrel-chested lifeguards would stand duty in their scuba equipment to chase off sharks or barracuda and to warn swimming guests against moray eels, sea anemones, sharp coral, and other perils to their exposed paunches.

The "Subhotel" would have a swimmers' launch room where the pressure would equal the sea pressure at that depth. This would serve as a kind of beach, with smooth sand spread along a sizable surface of water, through which guests would enter and leave for their skin-diving forays. After a day of exploring the reefs, sunken vessels, and the Disneyland amusement park for the kids, guests would have large public rooms to relax in, with great picture windows to prevent any feeling of claustrophobia. Underwater ballet outside could be interspersed with movies and other shows inside. Transportation to and from land could be accomplished by a jumbo-sized sub with a port at one end which would mate with the port of the "Subhotel." The mating procedure would resemble that of two capsules docking in space.

A "Subhotel" vacation would offer a total change from whatever tourists normally do. The weather would be 100 percent sure to be fair, the undesirable air quality reading would be zero, and it would always be quiet—unless The Machine should stop.

The United States Navy's three Sealabs in the 1960s sent a series of "aquanauts" to live in steel, pressurized seabed chambers. They stayed down for increasingly extended periods to learn how to stay fit and functional. Unfortunately one man was killed accidentally, and the program was discontinued. But NOAA in 1971 took over this kind of study, to start a "National Shallow Water Habitat Program." So far they haven't mixed genders in their experiments. Before the first Davy Jones Motel opens there of course has to be some advance knowledge of whether submarine cohabitation leads to any new tactics in the war between the sexes. But the technology is nearly ready, I'd say, for Hilton Hotels to go underseas with the next hotel they add to their chain, and to call it the Nautilus Hilton.

The Perfect City

Since the lost days of the Garden of Eden our species has tried to construct the perfect human settlement. For hundreds of years the design of towns featured protective walls inside which self-contained units of humanity could live indefinitely during sieges.

Schemes for breaking into these habitats from the outside have made some interesting history. The Trojan horse ruse worked fine for a one-shot. American Indians found that arrows with fiery tips would occasionally burn down stockades. And the Laotian capital of Vientiane, where I once lived, got its name (which some say means "wall of gold") because of a trick reputedly played on the inhabitants by the Thais, who had laid siege to the city: The cupidity of the Laotians being well known, the Thais shot a heavy fusillade of gold-tipped arrows into the city's walls, where they stuck. Soon the Laotians, according to legend, began pulling down their own walls to get the gold; and the Thais marched joyfully in.

The Roman village came close to perfection, back during the days of simple technology. Farms, houses, buildings for artisans, schools, theaters, public baths, military defense installations, and centers of local government were all within walking distance for the towns' inhabitants.

France's present government has been studying the way the Romans laid out these villages and is in the process of reproducing a modern version of what they call the "Latin village." At last report very little construction had been done at Vaudreuil, the experimental town. But the French hope it will demonstrate how to exploit the principles used so successfully by the Romans and combine them with modern techniques in a nonpolluted, noncrowded Utopia. Agriculture, industry, school, culture, recreation and local government will all be integrated so that each citizen can lead a full, balanced life without ever having to go anyplace he can't reach by walking. The plans include many ingenious innovations to assure an unblemished quality of life: For example, the smoke from the oil-burning power plant and factories will be carried away through tunnels and released in open fields many miles downwind of the town. One reason for the delay in getting on with the Vaudreuil project is doubtless the need to persuade the citizenry who live downwind of the tunnel's dirty end that the experiment is acceptable.

George Washington wanted a perfect capital for his brand new country and called in the French engineer Pierre L'Enfant. If L'Enfant's plan had been adhered to up to recent years, Washington might enjoy today much cleaner air than it does. Unfortunately hundreds of acres of the Potomac River have yielded to landfill. This has brought floods in the spring, the loss of wetlands, and a loss of water surface to cool and clean the city's ambient air, not to mention the extra miles of roads built on this landfill, accommodating additional numbers of automobiles with their poisonous emissions. It also ruined the view from the White House, which used to extend unobstructed many miles down the Potomac.

Two modern cities designed in recent years have so far managed to stave off the ecological deterioration that has befallen Washington: They are the capitals of Brazil (Brasilia) and Australia (Canberra). I have visited both of these lovely, broad-avenued, stately buildinged, industryless urban El Dorados. They each boast large, handsome artificial lakes and populations of people and automobiles that are rather undersized for the available residential and other facilities. A sprawling squatters' subcity of several thousand poor encroaches on and blights the limits of Brasilia. The answer to this tragic juxtaposition of urban life at its best and its worst still eludes the Brazilians.

A final note on these two urban paragons: Possibly because they were built all at once—in toto—both Brasilia and Canberra suffer from an antiseptic lack of personality. Maybe "It takes a heap o' livin' in a house t' make it home" applies to cities, too. So far, neither one offers much fun or warmth within its elegant boundaries. Still both are kind to the weather and the climate around them.

Encapsulated Cities

The fastest, surest path to change your personal weather is to put a roof over your head. Even a screen roof will do (as you can see in the age-old gardens of Lisbon, which are sheltered by a sunscreen scores of acres in size) or transparent glass (as greenhouses have demonstrated ever since glass was invented hundreds of years ago). Now the once humble roof is evolving glamorously into a key role in a revolutionary new kind of artificial environment, sheltered by such constructions as Buckminster Fuller's geodesic dome.

The new vogue for such enclosed environments has begun; and already it has many forms—inflatable buildings, for example. Bubbles over tennis courts, hockey rinks, and swimming pools can be erected with air pumps, permitting these sports to be enjoyed regardless of the weather outside. Enclosed stadia like the Houston Astrodome are likewise protecting both fans and players from the whims of weather.

More significant, though, is the new building that houses the Ford Foundation headquarters right in the middle of New York City. Its roof and southern wall are constructed of glass; and the area enclosed is so large that it encompasses a miniature city built literally indoors. Large trees and plants and a jungle pool stand in the vast eleven-story front portion of the structure. They are so beautifully arranged that to be there is to transpose oneself mystically to the lush tropical forest of William H. Hudson's entrancing book *Green Mansions*.[7]

The Ford building is the first small-scale showcase of how to put a whole city under glass. The now destroyed Pennsylvania Railroad Station in New York was an earlier, larger example, but it has to be discounted because it hadn't solved the problem of air quality control as has the Ford headquarters: There the atmosphere is fully thermostatted and filtered.

Technologically it is already feasible to encapsulate an entire city under a glass roof, thus avoiding bad climate and pollution at one brilliant stroke. How to enclose the power plants, factories, automobiles, and intransigent inhabitants who don't want to be stuck under glass are the "impossibilities" that will "take a little longer." But all these obstacles are surmountable technically; it's the cost problems that will probably take the longest to solve.

Assuming the city of Dallas, for example, could put on a glass hat, control of the temperature under the hat would be a prime consideration. This could be achieved by jalousie-type shades that would open and shut to harness the radiation of the sun, or exclude it. Harnessed radiation could supply a great proportion of the electricity needed for lights, endless-belt people movers, elevators, and escalators—which would replace automobiles.

Supplies in and out of the city could be handled by electric trains or trucks. Additional power requisites could be met by burning fossil fuels; their smoke and gases would be pumped out and exhausted some fifteen or twenty miles from the city, as in the French Vaudreuil experiment. Fresh air could be brought in occasionally by giant windows that could open at positions that would cause cross-drafts, as they do in today's houses; the quality of the air could be maintained by using filters, as done on submarines.

With a predictable climate inside the city, many vegetables and fruits could be raised there, thus saving transportation.

Once the big roof was in place then the cursed *non*opening windows and air conditioners for all the existing buildings could be removed. They would no longer be needed, since the over-all air temperature and cleanliness of the city would be regulated at a comfortable 75 degrees of dirt-free, elysium springtime. Gradually the architecture of the buildings, both for industry and for offices, could be more open, simpler, and less massive, since there would be no need to contend with excessive temperatures, winds, clouds, and precipitation. Overcoats and hats and heavy clothes would give way to the lightest garments; perhaps even nudism would become widely accepted. At the present cost of clothing, it would pay to shed needless pruderies!

Of course if the people of Dallas were to relinquish all their defenses against the natural elements, they would want to be sure that the system replacing them is dependable. Maintaining all the hardware to produce a heavenly climate citywide would require a tip-top professional department of electricians, mechanics, plumbers, and other technicians—in short, the kind of services that have been weakening seriously in this country. We should be leery of repeating the experience of that eighteen-story university building in Hamburg, Germany, which is fitted out with venetian blinds that cover every square inch of the glass that comprises the four sides of the building. The blinds are hooked up to a regulator that is fully automated with photosensors; they are supposed to close when the sun strikes them and open when the sun is gone. However, the hapless tenants were plagued from the first day of their occupancy by a total foul-up: The blinds opened and shut constantly all day long with absolutely no relationship to the position of the sun.

If encapsulating a complete social unit such as a city seems too advanced to be practical, we should take note of the tent caterpillar, who has done the job for millennia without a hitch. So have locusts and bees and "daubers" (hornets and wasps). Actually the achievement of these remarkable insects may encourage us to try affixing human settlements to mountainsides.

For those who want to escape the city, real estate enterprises might merchandise single or multiple family units stuck every few hundred feet or so from above the timber line to the top of Mount Everest. Robert O. Blake, a United States ambassador and long-legged hiking member of the 1976 Everest expedition, said that temporary shelters of this nature have been attempted already. The problems most evasive of solution have been the difficulty of getting food and other supplies up to the inhabitants, on the one hand; and on the other, the psychological "critical mass"—the question of how many people can stand each other for more than a few days under the abnormal conditions. Life support requirements such as pressurized air and moderated temperatures have all been perfected by the aerospace industry. Because of the ice, construction would be difficult, to put it mildly; but it is at least theoretically possible to drill holes in the rock beneath the ice and drive in steel foundations.

Such human aeries are bound to come, experimentally at first, and then for special purposes later. (SSTs are not yet commercially feasible either—or necessary—but because man could conceive of them we already have them.) Some future Hitler may want (and be able to afford) a Berchtesgaden niche well above the tourist line of a precipitous peak. Meteorologists would be ecstatic with mountainside laboratories in the sky, which might in fact speed up our lagging knowledge of the weather machine. Indeed, government research will probably provide the first living space at 29,000 feet.

Cities in the Sea

Since Noah took his community to sea two by two, man has often been tempted to shift his abode to floating quarters, at least during voyages. A change in the weather is always refreshing, and now that so many of our seaside resorts are befouled with overpopulation, overurbanization, and superpollution, a permanent berth at sea has special appeal.

Athelstan Spilhaus, at the ready per usual with ideas for new uses of the ocean, has offered artistic renderings of an actual city built to float on the sea and support a large number of people.

This concept has had more technological testing than cities

under glass or underwater. Since the turn of the century steamers have offered a way of life that can be semipermanent for the rich. Posh accommodations on the British liners which once went back and forth from England to India—"posh" stood for "Port Out, Starboard Home"—meant having your deck chair located at the proper place so as to catch the sun every afternoon of the long trip. More recently the navy's battleships and aircraft carriers keep thousands of men aboard for months at a time with no comfort missing except alcoholic beverages and the kindly presence of women. But all these cities at sea bring their passengers home once in a while—except the Flying Dutchman.

On Christmas Eve in 1976 I looked out to sea about eight P.M. from my house on a rocky beach of Newport, Rhode Island. Out of the black rose a vision which made me doubt my sanity. There on the horizon stood a city, lights ablaze; and from it rose a holiday tree hundreds of feet high sprinkled with brightly lit colored bulbs. A glance through my spyglass confirmed that the sight was real. A few minutes passed and the "city" had moved a mile or so to the east. An hour later all but the "tree" was hull down. What was this? Coney Island's garish version of the holy pageant? In the morning it had returned to its former spot about ten miles offshore. By then I had guessed what it was: The first gigantic floating oil drill rig we'd read about had arrived on station. The "tree" was the drilling tower. These floating monsters are the first real cities at sea. From them it is but a hop, skip, and a multibillion-dollar jump to the Spilhaus "home away from all homes."

He and others envisage several square miles of city, mounted on tall cylindrical legs like the latest oil drill platforms. Spilhaus envisions that the raison d'être for the first such city will be to serve as the locale for refineries and nuclear power plants that are rejected by environmentalists who want to preserve shoreline ecology.

I would suggest that the first city might start as a university town. This would mean a minimum of industry, with the businesses mainly of the service variety; and a population consisting largely of the younger, more flexible types. This city would serve as prototype for later, larger models. The shape of the floating settlement would be roughly oblong, with a kidney-shaped harbor cut on the leeward side, away from the prevailing winds. A small airfield would be located on the windward side to provide runways allowing the shortest possible takeoffs. The buildings would be kept to less than ten stories in order to avoid concentrating too much weight at any one point. Also it will be important to streamline the skyline of the city to minimize the "sail effect," so that prevailing breezes will not push the city along at a speed faster than its motive power can regulate. Landscaping would be done with rugged plants and bushes that grow in Scotland or New England perennials such as black pine and Rosa rugosa, which will hold their foliage in the worst of winds.

For cutting food costs, aquaculture would be practiced in enclosed sea areas under the city platform. For the enclosure, nets could be superseded by bubble barriers. These have been tested as effective; they are formed by placing pipes at the bottom of the enclosed area, with perforations in them every few inches. Air pumped through the pipes makes bubbles, which rise to form a fence all the way to the surface. Fish and marine vegetables would provide staple foods for the sea-city dwellers. Gardens for land vegetables could also be set up on the surface of the platform, in the lee of special wind walls erected for their protection.

Most of the power necessary for running the city would be derived from wave pulsators under the platform, which would ride up and down on the wave tops and be geared to reciprocating pistons. These could drive electrical generators. Large propellers set in the ocean at strategic points along the edges of the city could move the city along at three knots, or could keep it locked in one place. If a stay in one place for longer than a few days were desired, anchors could be dropped. Command of the floating island city would alternate among towers located at each of the platform's four corners, depending on the direction in which the city might be moving. Presumably—at least in the days before civilization builds so many of these cities that there is an oceanic space problem—they will stay in the latitudes where the weather is most congenial to human tastes.

Dr. Spilhaus lays out a delightful schedule for riding the Gulf Stream for a full year on one of these roving islands: Start the sequence by moving into the Gulf Stream to pass the winter off Florida; float up to New England for the late spring; then over to England for the summer; in the fall, down to the west coast of Africa; and for the winter, back to the environs of Miami once more.

Dr. Spilhaus also would employ such cities in the extraction and processing of bauxite into aluminum. This is very messy business; but the disposal problem which plagues manufacturers on the land would be nonexistent at sea. The spoils could be dropped on the deep ocean bed where there is little biological activity to be interfered with. Making aluminum is also energy-intensive, but the wave pulsators could handle the load, according to Spilhaus.

In June of 1976 some hundred scientists, engineers, and sociologists assembled at Airlie House in Virginia to examine the worthwhileness of man's moving to sea in such cities. NOAA, MARAD (the Maritime Administration), and other organizations sponsored the session. Athelstan Spilhaus was honorary chairman. The outcome was a positive prognosis from the sages whose professional standing entitles them to express an opinion on such futuristic matters.

The sea, comprising over 70 percent of the earth's surface, should be able to carry as many of these cities as man can afford, with all of them under the horizon from each other. They might multiply to include retirement settlements for the wealthy, then floating company towns for industry, then perhaps strings of cities to house the diverse industries of conglomerates.

With the latest "laws" of the sea establishing 200-mile areas offcoast within which nations can pursue economic and geological development, these cities can serve to establish national presences in such areas. Also they can serve as mining and processing centers for picking up the millions of manganese nodules which lie on many portions of the seabed, ready for the taking. These cities will probably have to operate over the abyssal depths when they're away from the coasts of their mother country. Since they will be sitting ducks for any nuclear attack, they will have to be "woolly bears" politically. Assuming such cities become numerous, it will be good to have large populations who are so vulnerable they can't entertain any aggressive intent. Since their cities will have to stay at sea forever—no coastal port would suffice to berth them—one day they might foolishly complicate their blissful freedom by declaring their independence of their mother countries—but one hopes that maritime mayors would be able to defuse such movements!

Colonies Anchored in the Sky

"Star Trek" is poised to move from our TV sets to a fixed point equidistant from the earth and the moon, if you believe Dr. Gerard K. O'Neill, a Princeton University physicist. If we want to pursue our quest for instant good weather to the ultimate in sophisticated engineering, that's where we've got to go. To be viable, every community must have a purpose; and the task of Professor O'Neill's space colony would be to tend huge, orbiting, solar-power relay stations, which would be beaming microwave radiation to the earth for conversion there to electricity.

But if the idea proves practicable the number of colonies could be multiplied as a drain-off mechanism to ease this planet's overpopulation, energy shortages, and environmental degradation.

Those who want details galore on this inventive scheme should read Dr. O'Neill's book *High Frontier*.[8] In a word, he envisages gigantic, hollow cylinders miles long and perhaps two miles in diameter. These would be constructed from metal mined on the moon. Complete earth-type landscapes would line the inside of the cylinders. Hills and rills and lakes and fields would be created, just like those God put on the earth in Genesis. Towns would follow.

To do all this, soil, rock, and atmosphere would be derived mostly from moon materials and passing asteroids. Minerals from moon mines could be extracted far more cheaply than those from the earth, because of lighter gravity both at the ore site and in transport to the cylinders. For human comforts, gravity in the cylinders would be increased to approximate parity with that on earth by rotating them. Sunlight could be controlled by admitting it via swiveling mirrors. The biosphere within could sustain thousands, maybe millions of humans living under what the scientists call "baseline" conditions—the conditions that prevailed on earth before man began to tear them apart. (In O'Neill's orbiting world, "baseline" would be the moment man completed its construction.) Inhabitants and their baggage would travel from earth to the colony by NASA's space shuttle, now being tested.

In projecting what existence will be like in these colonies (which O'Neill predicts could become so numerous that earth's population might actually be diminished in a century or so) O'Neill allows the mind to play with all manner of intriguing possibilities. For example, he hints at the easy joy connubial partners would find at bedtime with the low gravity prevailing in some parts of the colony.

I suppose it was inevitable that the United States feat of putting Armstrong's feet on the moon would be followed by a plan like Dr. O'Neill's. What is surprising is that a hundred scientists, engineers, lawyers, and sociologists met in Princeton in 1975 and concluded that what Dr. O'Neill has in mind *is* practicable with existing technology. They say it may occur as he foresees it, within this generation.

How seriously should we view the prospects for this space world created by man? One brilliant geophysicist dismissed it with, "Can we really construct a truly self-sustaining artificial biosphere anywhere in space? An artist's illustration shows streams running, sunshine, and clouds and people happily at their daily rounds. Isn't the whole idea blasphemous? Aren't we really competing with *Him*?"

Joseph E. Karth, long-time chairman of the House of Representatives subcommittee on the unmanned space flight program, exploded when I queried him. "It wasn't worthy of holding a hearing on. It's an insane dream and completely outrageous as to cost. It took over twenty billion dollars just to send one man to the moon on the Apollo series; one and a half billion to send an unmanned ship to Mars; and ten billion to maybe fifteen billion to develop one rather small space shuttle. But the colony concept is absolutely crazy—these are mad people. If they were in charge of operating our government they'd spend the total income of this country for the next twenty years—all our money for that period— and still never finish the project. There's not enough money in the whole world to do it."

"What if all the nations banded together the way the ants do to make a huge anthill?" I asked.

"Well, if all the industrialized nations got together and put their finest engineers and scientists to work on it, and if you could forget all the people and what they need to live . . . well, it might be just remotely possible from a technological standpoint."

"How come all those scientists endorsed its practicality at Princeton?" I pursued.

"Because they have tunnel vision when something of this sort comes up. There never were any scientists we asked who were against any space program. They always said it could be done."

"Maybe if even a limited go-ahead could be given, then the money would start flowing again at NASA—is that what they may be hoping?"

"Exactly," he nodded.

Nevertheless, the Senate subcommittee on aerospace technology did give Dr. O'Neill a hearing in 1976. They listened politely. Also, I have contacted people in the aerospace industry, including its association president, Karl Harr. The feeling I end with is that this concept is out of the ball park for implementation right now. But we still should pursue and examine and investigate it and not just reject it out of hand.

For those who care about conditions back here on earth, I don't think we should be diverted from them by Dr. O'Neill's delightful plot to rescue us from the mess we've made. If we choose to stay home for good weather, there are hopes for us in the future, even on this tired old earth.

Artificial Environments May Be Good for You

Finally, there is a physical plus to providing good weather, such as in the artificial habitats mentioned here. I have seen that air conditioning can raise a person's capacity for endurance in the severe extremes of tropical climate at posts I held during my foreign service for the United States government. In Laos and the Congo, during the days when they belonged to France and Belgium, respectively, the colonial masters had to return to Europe every six months for at least three months of physiological battery charging. Yet by the time these colonies became independent nations, when the United States set up embassies there with new, air-conditioned, and comfortable buildings, American personnel were able to stick it out for full two-year tours and return to the United States on home leave healthy and fit. Even in Israel, I noticed that at the end of the long hot season the Sabras (native Israelis) without air conditioners in their houses and offices began to get sick and stayed weak until the fall months cooled off the country. In Israel, too, the Americans stayed well throughout the year.

If this experience can be extrapolated to apply a kind of guaranteed good weather for entire communities (which is what we would be creating in our cities in the sea, or underseas, or under glass, or even in the sky) then not only our day-to-day health might benefit, but also our life span. By removing us from the wear and tear of climatic extremes, artificial environments might prepare the human race for a longevity that is only dreamed of in our generation. So there is reason to further these efforts at creating artificial environments.

PART TWO

ENVIRONMENTAL MODIFICATION: NEGATIVE

5

ENVIRONMENTAL WARFARE

Literature has long recognized the violent aspects of the environment, from Shakespeare's *The Tempest* to Emily Brontë's *Wuthering Heights,* in which the hero Heathcliffe personifies the aggressive, wild wind of the Scottish Moors. As for the military role of the environment, the ancient scribes wrote about it when recounting the Greek and biblical myths in which deities directed natural forces against evildoers. In the Old Testament the Red Sea parts when Moses is leading his people to the Promised Land; and the pursuing Egyptians rush onto the sea bottom to pursue the retreating Jews only to have the waters surge back and drown them:

> And Moses stretched forth his hand over the sea, and the sea returned to his strength and overthrew the Egyptians in the midst of the sea. And the waters returned, and covered the chariots, and the horsemen, and all the host of Pharaoh that came into the sea after them; there remained not so much as one of them.[1]

Later, in more conventionally recorded history, we can read how military forces took advantage of the environment to win battles. As Roman ships bore down on Syracuse during one of the Punic Wars, Archimedes is said to have stopped the Romans with polished shields, like a giant mirror, focusing the sun on the sails of the warships so that the canvas burst into flame.

"Scorched earth" is one of the oldest tactics of environmental warfare: denying the invading army the means to live off the land. The Russians perfected it against the hordes of both Napoleon and Hitler. In "scorching the earth," they removed trees and housing the enemy might use for shelter, crops and animals and food stores and forage for feeding enemy troops and their horses, gas and oil for the tanks and trucks and planes of Hitler. General Sherman employed the same strategy against the Confederacy by laying waste a wide swath from Atlanta to Savannah.

We now hear of more exotic environmental weapons in fiction and in the press. Can we believe, for example, that some malevolent cabal has been, or could be, making the so-called Bermuda Triangle into an atmospheric-oceanic quicksand in which the unwitting traveler sinks inexplicably? Perhaps, as some have suggested, the Bermuda Triangle victims are disappearing into some sort of fourth dimension designed by an enemy.

We have to assume that the dirty tricks departments and weapons development experts in any alert nation must be examining any and all possibilities for self-defense in this treacherous world. Even terrorists may be toying with the idea of eco-war if it proves practicable for short time spans.

Robert White, administrator of NOAA, has ultimate responsibility for most federal programs of weather modification and he sees no purpose in spending money for military applications in peacetime. When war comes, he points out, there's virtually no environmental modification activity that can't be redirected for national defense. In any case, says Dr. White, environmental warfare is "madness." Almost all other scientists tend to share White's view.

We know how we tried to bring a halt to Communist mobility in Vietnam by rainmaking and even mudmaking. Chemical weaponry is still another branch of environmental warfare, for it poisons the breeze that wafts toward the opposing army. Mustard and chlorine gases were brought into the fighting in World War I—with a mixed record, since the wind direction is never totally dependable. To my knowledge, neither side used this sinister capability during the Vietnam struggle, although United States forces did employ tear gas with the abandon of riot police. Ultimately it became the most effective single device for flushing enemy soldiers out of hiding.

Representative Donald M. Fraser, along with Gilbert Gude, held hearings in 1974 on House resolutions calling on the United States government to seek international agreements to limit the deployment of weather modification as a weapon of war. There were two particularly strong pieces of testimony, one positive, one negative.

Dr. Edith Brown Weiss of Princeton University hit out positively at the whole idea of environmental war. Her main points were that weather modification techniques are unpredictable in their effects. She said: "Either individually or together they could trigger irreversible changes in weather and climate, which no state could control. Hostile uses are more likely than other uses to get out of control, because decisions will be made on the basis of military exigencies, with . . . little regard for environmental considerations." She said that environmental warfare "may affect the weather of nearby neutral states"; would involve an attack on civilians which would "violate international law"; would "further undermine the already shaky distinction between conventional and unconventional means of warfare" and would legitimize environmental modification as a weapon of war ("This is particularly undesirable in a world which is becoming increasingly vulnerable to unconventional means of warfare"); and would cast suspicion on the development and use of such technology for peaceful purposes. Dr. Weiss said, "If one state develops and uses these techniques for hostile purposes she invites others to do so."

Admiral Thomas D. Davies, on the other hand, basically poohpoohed the whole idea of environmental war. He said that "any attempts to modify the earth's climate or the climate of a region, for peaceful or hostile purposes, are simply theoretical. . . . Similarly of a theoretical nature are capabilities to divert ocean currents, cause tsunamis or tidal waves, trigger earthquakes, or modify the ionosphere in any large-scale way." Yet the admiral had to concede that the possiblilities of success have been evaluated as high enough to warrant continued research.

With no disrespect intended, I wonder if the admiral was giving his own opinion, or simply following the policy of "no comment" that I have been running into elsewhere in my own independent inquiries.

Dr. Gordon J. F. MacDonald has been much more outgoing than most. MacDonald, now an environmental geophysicist at Dartmouth University, captivated readers in the sixties with his article "How to Wreck the Environment."[2] This imaginative inventory of far-out, maybe impracticable schemes goes farther than any other individual presentation on this subject in the sheer number of possibilities he discusses. MacDonald elaborated the hypothesis that in the earth and its atmosphere there are natural pressures that build up over time and that finally become unstable, with the kind of precarious stability we see in a human about to sneeze or to have an orgasm, or in a rock balanced on the edge of a cliff, or in that well-known overloaded camel on whose back just a tiny straw will finally destroy his carrying capacity.

The key to geophysical warfare, says MacDonald, is to identify those environmental instabilities to which the addition of a small amount of energy will release vastly greater energy. He describes dramatic "for instances"—weather modification to start with. He reminds us that such weather phenomena as tornados, thunderstorms, or hurricanes contain so much energy that it is unlikely puny man can move them around by any ordinary force. Only by looking for their pressure points or "meteorological erogenous zones," so to speak, can we find a handle to manage them by. Though we made rain in the Vietnam war, harnessing a hurricane is something no one has tried. But MacDonald hints it's possible.

If we could steer hurricanes against hostile territory we could frighten the enemy, kill people, and smash property. MacDonald doesn't spell out the steering method other than to say "various schemes for both dissipation and steering can be imagined"; however, he provides a clue: the use of monomolecular films, like oil or oily compounds, which sometimes are laid on the surface of reservoirs to prevent evaporation. These could be stretched over ocean spaces to intercept the flow of energy from the warm water into the atmosphere and thus decelerate the growth of a hurricane. Coordinate this action with selected cloud seeding, suggests MacDonald, and you might have the basic elements of a steering mechanism.

MacDonald goes on to examine theories of various inventive scientists for waging environmental war. Yet his examples seem to require brute force rather than the finger on the trigger; and he himself acknowledges the need for more knowledge and power in order to bring most of them to reality. He recounts such schemes as sliding the ice off the Antarctic continent. This is theoretically doable because the great thickness of the ice (about 10,000 feet) puts the footing under great pressure, tending to melt it. A nuclear explosion or two might encourage the melting and the great load of ice might crumble and slide into the sea. If this happened, then a greater area of the sea would be topped with white;* and this would reflect more heat away from the earth and cool the area for a while. The climate change might be disadvantageous to Argentina, at least until the extended ice melted. MacDonald estimates the ice might take forty years to move all the way from the Antarctic to the mainland.

Another act of environmental war would be to detonate nuclear explosions under the bedrock at the edge of the continental shelf, knocking a huge chunk off into the adjacent abyssal (deep) sea and thus sending a tidal wave going toward unfriendly shores.

How about an earthquake made to order? As mentioned in chapter 3, we have discovered how to trigger one. We now know that if you know the location of a geophysical fault running through

---

* This would occur because the ice-vacated land would soon be snow-covered again because of normal, continuing precipitation.

a city, and if you can inject water into it or set off a subterranean bomb in it without getting caught, and if you have a sufficient military motive to do all this, you might be able to pull off a repeat of the devastating San Francisco, Tokyo, China, or Guatemala quakes. A lot of *ifs*.

There is a more or less continuous fault line on the edges of the countries that border the Pacific Basin. Beneath the fault line there is magma—molten lava—under great pressure. If one could release the friction that seals the faults and let the lava up, shaking the earth, he could not only demolish cities but also set off destructive tsunamis (great sea waves) when the quakes occur alongside the sea.

The mid-Atlantic rift is another likely spot for troublemaking. This mountain range along the central Atlantic's bottom is thought still to contain tremendous pressures, probably the same ones that threw up the mountains originally. The earth's crust is thinner under the sea; and if you could puncture it—as a doctor lances a boil—either by drilling or by explosions, you might give rise to another "instant island" like Surtsey, which popped through the ocean floor near Iceland a few years ago. At least you could make a quake.

Why bother? Well, it's conceivable there might be unfriendly foreigners in the Atlantic, tapping oil deposits or extracting magnesium nodules, and you might wish to interrupt them.

Perhaps my observations on environmental war may seem unseemly and jocose given the potential seriousness of the subject, but the Soviets think it may well come to reality, particularly weather warfare. Their scientists believe man can make windows in the ozone belt which may fry to a crisp the animal, vegetable, and human life on the earth below. MacDonald gives this theory some credence. He confirms that a hole in the ozone layer might be cut by physical or chemical action: Ultraviolet rays could be beamed at the layer to decompose ozone molecules, and the resulting atoms could be exposed to any one of a wide range of substances with which they might combine.

Soviet Ambassador Jacob A. Malik, at the United Nations General Assembly in 1975, stated that the USSR fears that environmental war-makers could create acoustical fields on the ocean surface to immobilize ships; or set off nuclear explosions inside the polar ice caps producing ice slides which, hitting the sea, would start "tidal waves capable of wiping whole areas from the face of the globe."

One of the oldest Sunday supplement nightmares of geophysical warfare is that some world power might sneak under the Gulf Stream and build a giant undersea dam to divert it away from the continent of Europe back toward Greenland. If the New World were engaged in fighting with the Old World, this plan might make sense. Such a shift of the Gulf Stream would deliver to Greenland the heat it picked up in tropical latitudes, and convert the island's climate back to the one it enjoyed when Leif Ericson gave it its name. Meanwhile, the present temperate zone of Europe, including Scandinavia, would slip back into an Ice Age and lose its military and industrial might. The trouble with the theory is its probable total impossibility because of the size of the Gulf Stream, and the enormous dimension and strength of any dam that would suffice to change the Stream's course.

Various scientists like Gordon J. F. MacDonald and Athelstan Spilhaus have noodled about using the ionosphere as a vehicle to transmit disruptive electrical waves into human brains. Spilhaus disposes lightly of the thought that human behavior can be influenced in this manner. When the atmosphere is charged with negative ions, he says, some doctors think people are cheered up, while positive ions lower their spirits. In a cartoon from his science series "The New Age,"[3] a couple giving a buffet party says, "Let's turn up the ionostat; everybody at the party looks bored!" MacDonald explores the concept of electrical control over the brain in more detail and suggests that manipulating lightning strokes might be used to send oscillations of specific frequencies from the ionosphere to influence people's behavior:

> . . . tropical thunderstorms are always available for manipulation. The proper geographical location of the source of lightning, coupled

with accurately timed, artificially executed strikes, could lead to a pattern of oscillations that produced relatively high power levels over certain regions of the earth and substantially lower levels over other regions. In this way one could develop a system that would seriously impair brain performance in very large populations in selected regions over an extended period.[4]

In this way, MacDonald concludes, the military leaders of one nation might be able to degrade the performance of large populations in other nations, if they found it in their nation's interest to do so. MacDonald concedes that such weird capability seems hard to accept at present; nevertheless, "technology permitting, such use will very probably develop within the next few decades."[5]

The way microwaves have been leaking into the ionosphere in recent years may mean the technology for electrical mind control is racing to the forefront right now. Way back in World War II the Japanese army was investigating the possibility of using microwaves as a death ray, but the results of the study were destroyed by fire in 1945. Now the effectiveness of microwaves as a long-range weapon is beginning to be seen.

Microwaves radiate out from microwave ovens (some 200,000 of them, as of now), from radar installations, from control mechanisms of the antiballistic missile system, from buried shortwave communications systems designed to keep in touch with our nuclear subs at the bottom of the sea, and from a couple of mysterious sources in the Soviet Union. Paul Brodeur's intriguing two-part series in the *New Yorker,* December 1976, elaborates vividly what is happening.[6] The war potential of microwaves is touched on several times in Brodeur's articles: Mircrowaves probably cause cataracts in overexposed humans; microwave alteration of the blood-brain barrier can lead to neuropathic symptoms in human victims, who may die or may suffer neural impairment; or can affect the rhythm of the heartbeat or cause it to stop altogether (this learned from an experiment with cats).

As the harmfulness of microwaves becomes better understood,

doubtless the possibility will increase that they can be directed purposely over long distances, to injure humans or cause them to act in self-destructive patterns. The still unexplained incident of microwave bombardment of the United States Embassy in Moscow might be considered an early warning of this possibility.

In conclusion, war by environment seems rather fanciful and illusory at this writing, with two exceptions:

First, there are rather well perfected techniques available for dispersing cold fog, either in order to expose bombing targets for an attacking air force or in order to clear the flight deck of an aircraft carrier or a landing field ashore. Some have estimated, for example, that World War II might have ended weeks earlier if the Allies could have swept away heavy clouds by the various means we now have for that purpose.

Second, my guess is that most modern defense departments are bound to have looked into the field of environmental warfare, and come up with at least contingency plans for employing environmental weaponry in wartime. Given the ingenuity of our civilization and the fantastic resources at hand today in science and technology, no one knows all that lurks in the minds of those charged with their country's security.

As might be expected, I have been unable to determine exactly what is going on, although our own Department of Defense's announced policy is that all research and development will be handled on a strictly nonclassified basis.

However, I do not believe that the allegations of Lowell Ponte are accurate when in his book *The Cooling*[7] he hints that the Department of Defense has the necessary meteorological magic to degrade at long distance the agricultural productivity of the Soviet Union, the People's Republic of China, and Cuba. Able scientists deny such magic exists.

On the other hand doesn't our Defense Department owe us, as taxpayers, the vigilance and know-how to determine whether any such capability does exist, in case some other nation may be planning to use it against us at this very moment?

There is strong conviction among some meteorologists such as Gordon MacDonald that a campaign of weather warfare could be launched by one country against another in total secrecy. If successful, the attacking nation could simply reply to any victim who complains, "Why, don't be silly; weather is unpredictable. The bad storms, drought, and floods that are plaguing you stem only from the vagaries of nature."

6

UNINTENDED WAR ON WEATHER, CLIMATE, AND ENVIRONMENT

For over six years at EPA I watched the environment stagger under its load of pollutants, from a perspective not readily available to my fellow countrymen. To me, the experience has been like that when I first saw live organisms under a microscope in the school laboratory—it has made me uneasy. At fifteen I was just beginning to get the hang of controlling my life and the elements that affected it. But how could I defend myself against those lively microscopic creatures that were invisible to the naked eye?

Watched from my EPA vantage, recent happenings to our environment remind me of the Robert Louis Stevenson story about Dr. Jekyll and Mr. Hyde, which could be a parable for our time. There are already signs that filth in our environment may distort it one day as the sinister potion did Dr. Jekyll.

In Stevenson's book Jekyll is a decent, healthy physician who experiments with a chemical compound that can evoke in the most innocent human his innate tendency toward evil. On swallowing the potion as a test, Jekyll proves that it works: He swiftly metamorphoses into "Mr. Hyde," horribly ugly and the epitome of sin and corruption. But Jekyll has also prepared an antidote which allows him to resume his own uncorrupted personality and appearance. He feels secure that in the name of science he can pollute his clean self and then redeem it after each experiment, like a drunk sobering up.

Then one day tragedy strikes. Jekyll abruptly and involuntarily becomes Hyde *without* taking the formula; and the antidote no longer will bring Jekyll back.

This kind of disaster may be ahead for our environment, especially the climate. Our "air quality alerts" today are the result of *dirt,* dumped into the atmosphere like a foul potion by our cars, factories, power plants, and airplanes. So far, nature can still dispose of it—though in some cities it is taking longer and longer to do so. But one day soon, say some eminent scientists, pollution will without warning, become irreversible and will change our climate from a healthful Jekyll that nourishes and sustains us, to a murderous Hyde that attacks our very existence.

Man's Historic Way with the Environment

Our civilization has already reshaped *local* conditions in every corner of the globe by hunting, fishing, farming, deforestation, industrialization, and urbanization. We have changed the globe's air through pollution; its water, both by pollution and by building dams and canals; and also its fauna—witness the destruction of wild animals, fish, and birds.

History reveals man in an endless role as warrior—against his fellow man and against nature. We fight against both for the same reasons: first need, and then greed for more—more food, more raw materials, more territory, and more power.

We periodically make peace with our fellow travelers on the planet, but our struggle to exploit natural surroundings goes on unabated. Only in recent decades have we begun to see that in beating down our environment, we may be setting the stage for our own exit from the planet. At last, we have partially embraced conservation.

We are slowly realizing that we often injure the environment whether we mean to or not. In fact, we have for a long time unconsciously upset local climates. We have sinned against the self-perpetuating systems of nature in many places. The following locations I have seen firsthand in their present, mutilated condition. From reading books and other writings from the past I have pieced together an idea of how they once looked before they felt the cutting edge of civilization.

Let's start with the Sahara Desert. Around 1500 B.C. it sported a thick covering of grass and a healthy average rainfall. Then the nomads allowed their herds to overgraze and close-crop the green pastures; the grass died, and a desert was born.

The Mediterranean shores of North Africa also bore heavy forests, until the minions of the Greek and Roman empires felled the trees to build the ships for their daring campaigns of conquest. Spain's plains were also once wooded; and the rains did stay mainly there before the trees bowed to the ax and dry air replaced the earlier humidity.

Further east, in Israel's Negev Desert, the late, famous American archaeologist Nelson Glueck found myriad traces of tribes that tried to preserve, not destroy, the cultivable land there. The Nabateans around the time of Christ, and later the Byzantines, labored to save the scant annual rainfall with intricate networks of water terraces, catch basins, cisterns and reservoirs. Dr. Glueck describes in *Rivers in the Desert* [1] how these people managed to produce rich farms and create prosperous towns in what had long been thought to be an uninhabitably barren area. Glueck deduced this mostly through potsherds scattered around the desert surface in or under nondescript mounds ("tells") which signal the sites of the ancient, ruined towns.

While I was stationed at the United States embassy in Tel Aviv, Dr. Glueck took me on one of his Negev expeditions to collect evidence for his book. Also with us were a dozen kibbutzniks and

Israeli soldiers on leave. The Sabra (native-born Israeli) has a passionate interest in archaeology, so the popular, urbane Dr. Glueck never wanted for volunteer explorers to accompany him.

We were all impressed with the imaginative genius of this rabbi and college president* who had earlier found King Solomon's copper mines south of the Dead Sea. He could examine a pottery fragment and—poof!—like the genie from a bottle, whole cities would spring out of nowhere as he talked to us. They were real cities, too, for he knew the Bible and could quote passages that authenticated his findings in the desert.

Dr. Glueck ascribes the disappearance of these early civilizations from the Negev and nearby areas not to the vagaries of climate, as suggested by some historians, but to human behavior. ". . . The horrifying tendency of man, wearily repeated throughout the centuries, to take his neighbor's goods or country, or to 'scorch' the land for his own protection and his enemies' hurt, is all too adequate a reason. It certainly makes understandable why scores of cities have been reduced to piles of faceless rubble, rich countrysides transformed almost overnight into wildernesses . . ."[2] Dr. Glueck thus reminds us that environmental warfare started a long time ago.

The now barren hills of Iran, some say, got that way from the chomping of Alexander the Great's 50,000 horses which were gradually carrying his armies towards further triumphs farther east.

These scenes of desert making are being repeated today in the deforestation that is going on apace in Brazil, Thailand, and Borneo. Now there is a new twist: *reverse* desert making. This is creeping into the Arizona valley next to Phoenix in the form of lush new vegetation, nurtured by irrigation. Where the Arizonans formerly lived in dry, bearable air, they must now endure a wet, soggy, and hot atmosphere with thunderheads in the afternoons. This seems a step back from the healthful climate that once at-

* Dr. Glueck was president of Hebrew Union College, Cincinnati, Ohio.

tracted thousands of sickly tuberculosis patients, sinus sufferers, and people will allergies.

El Centro, California, orginally sauna-hot and comfortably dry, has gone wet and sticky from verdant growth watered by the Coachella and All-American canals. Does this signify a permanent change? Probably yes, as long as the precious gallons from the Colorado River keep gurgling through canals.

Some guessed Lake Nasser would bring a wetter climate to Egypt; but it hasn't. Recently, I asked an Aswan Dam maintenance scientist there if anyone had wanted to seed the clouds that drift overhead in order to induce a bit of rain. After all, I thought without saying so, this country is still mostly a desert.

"What do we want rain for?" he rebuked me cheerfully. "We've got the Nile."

Less cheerful were thirty prominent scientists in their 1972 *Study of Man's Impact on Climate* (SMIC).[3] Even with all their academic hedgings, these wise men forecast a gloomy future. By the end of the century, they wrote, the pileup of pollution will register permanent, dangerous mutations on the global climate.

American climatologists have come to similar conclusions. Some are pursuing this subject at the Lawrence Livermore Laboratory. The University of California runs the lab for the United States Energy Research and Development Administration.

As previously mentioned, its Atmospheric Sciences Division includes the talented Michael C. MacCracken—spotted as a "comer" by the lab's senior intellect, Edward Teller of hydrogen bomb fame.

Climate is MacCracken's business, but he is candid and humorous about its complexities. Ask him what climate is and he'll say "a conglomeration of meteorological anomalies." Ask him, "What's the difference between weather and climate?" He'll grin and tell you, "Climate is what you expect, and weather is what you get." But he stresses that climate's "norm" is so various that demonstrating man's traces on it is a tough task.

To differentiate, with some help from Webster: Weather is the condition of the atmosphere at any particular time; climate the average, or prevailing, weather over a period of time.

Current Unintended Threats to Environment and Climate

Nevertheless, MacCracken has evidence that we can and do inadvertently strain climatic balances whose loss could endanger our species. In this opinion he has much company.

THREATS TO OZONE LAYER

For openers, he warns, we may destroy the delicate fourteen-mile-deep ozone layer (figure 5). This is the loose collection of three-atom oxygen molecules in the stratosphere, which comprises only one part in four million of the air at this level. The ozone layer is so cotton-flimsy that if brought to sea level, the weight of the atmo-

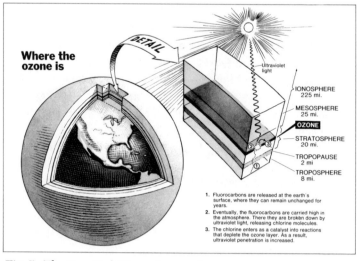

Fig. 5. (The New York Times Company)

sphere would compress it to the thickness of your finger. Ozone forms in the stratosphere when ultraviolet radiation from the sun meets oxygen. (Oxygen, 21 percent, and nitrogen, 78 percent, are the main components of the air which surrounds the earth.) This chemical reaction yields heat, and this produces a permanent temperature inversion in the stratosphere. This thermal ceiling retains the pollutants that float up there, just as the inversion lid over Los Angeles locks in the smog from car exhausts.

Fortunately, the ozone layer, formed by ultraviolet radiation (DUV) also prevents some of the ultraviolet rays from traveling down to the earth's surface. This filtering of the ultraviolet rays makes it possible for man to live, as well as the crops and animals on which he feeds, for ultraviolet rays can be lethal: They promote skin cancer in humans, inhibit photosynthesis, and stunt and kill plants and animals. They even interfere with the navigation and behavior of insects.

In short, we must not injure this ozone sunscreen in the sky, which protects life on the earth's surface below.

High-yield nuclear explosions in the atmosphere could weaken this protective ozone band, says MacCracken. The heat of one fireball, perhaps millions of degrees Fahrenheit, forms nitrogen oxides. If a bomb exceeds one megaton (one million tons of TNT) these oxides will bubble up through the troposphere—in which we live and which contains the air we breathe—to the stratosphere, which starts about twenty miles above the earth. There the oxides will disrupt the ozone chemically, since ozone is unstable and combines readily with nitrogen and chlorine compounds.

We don't yet know how many bombs—and of what size—would be necessary to consume the whole ozone belt. It has been calculated, however, that for each 1 percent decrease of ozone the increase in ultraviolet rays reaching the earth will be 2 percent. So it seems likely that a major nuclear exchange would release ample samples of the ozone-destroying nitrogen oxides. The humans who might survive the nuclear blasts, fire, and radioactivity would still face the hazard of increased ultraviolet emissions from the sun.

Even without a nuclear war, too much atmospheric testing of hydrogen bombs may well cause a dangerous depletion of the ozone cover.

Other substances also create the nitrogen oxides which rise to pepper the planet's ozone ramparts. Artificial fertilizers, for example, are now spread extensively in many emerging nations. High-flying supersonic aircraft also create nitrogen oxides. So far not many nitrogen oxides (in total) emanate from the British-French Concorde (of which there are less than a dozen) nor the Russian Turbolev 144 (of which there are only a few more). But some 10,000 supersonic military aircraft fly in the defense forces of industrialized nations, plus those nations like Israel, Iran, Saudi Arabia, and Kuwait whose airplanes are supplied by the United States or Europe.

We don't know what these airplanes do to our friendly ozone layer. Possibly not much, because they don't fly as often or for such lengthy periods as commercial transports—at least that's what the military say—unless there's a war on. Congress was told when it was weighing the merits of an American SST that it would damage the ozone layer. Paul Crutzen, a meteorologist at Stockholm University, said it in tougher language in 1974: A fleet of 500 SSTs flying at an altitude of 21 kilometers for 11 hours per day would peel off 12 percent of the ozone blanket globally, and 20 percent locally, that is, in the areas through which the planes would actually pass on any given flight.[4]

Here I will reflect a moment on my EPA dealings with the Concorde from 1974 to 1976. The French and British managers of the Concorde were making their preparations for the great day when they would reduce Europe-United States air service to a mere three hours. Their joyful anticipation was probably heightened by the fact that this would be the first major aeronautical breakthrough to be accomplished by Europeans rather than Americans since Blériot flew the British Channel in 1906. The combination ecological-economic offensive against the United States SST neatly eliminated America from the race for commercial supersonic primacy in 1971.

EPA was required to recommend to the Federal Aviation Administration what limits should be set on the noise levels for the new breed of aircraft. As to air emissions, EPA was empowered to issue its rules directly. Concorde leaders therefore wanted to be sure that EPA would have a fair and favorable understanding of Concorde's environmental impact. We in EPA also needed to know the facts before we could arrive at our own assessment.

Hence, we had many contacts with the Anglo-French Concorde team. Concorde personnel briefed me and our technical cognoscenti often, articulately and well, in my office in Washington, the American embassy, and the British government's offices in London, as well as the engine and assembly plants in England. Noise levels were tested at Dulles, New York, and Dallas-Fort Worth airports.

Our mingling with the Concorde people was often fraught with tension. For one thing President Nixon had assured the British and French leaders that the United States government would bend over backward to be just on the regulatory aspects of the proposed SST service. Our Concorde acquaintances were not averse to reminding EPA and the State Department of this fact. Some of our foreign policy advisors thought it likely that Concorde was in imminent danger of collapse because funds were running out. They cautioned that its fostering governments might want EPA and FAA to take prohibitively stiff regulatory actions so that these could be the scapegoat to absorb the rancor of British and French voters. In the middle of the discussions, there were elections resulting in new administrations in both Britain and France.

During this period, a British ecologist told me at lunch in our London embassy that as a former economist he had to say that in all of Britain's financial history, Concorde was unique: It was the only project on which money would have been saved if it were scrapped at any time—before, during, or after the moment at which it would commence scheduled flights.

One of the Concorde's French pilots, a darkly good-looking young fellow, recounted a more savory uniqueness about the superplane. He was relaxing at a lunch I gave in Washington, along with four EPA colleagues. Perhaps the California red wine we served encouraged him to speak freely. He said that during one takeoff he sat in the passenger cabin next to a lovely young lady, a guest of the airline. As the airship rapidly accelerated down the runway at Orly she suddenly rolled her eyes at him with a rather feverish expression. A few seconds later she sought his hand with hers. Then at the peak G of the roaring, thrusting takeoff her eyes closed, she moaned, cried out in the pain of pleasure, and clutched his hand pulsatingly and hard. "What power!" she exclaimed. "Kiss me!"

"How are you Yanks going to regulate that?" he demanded, his eyes snapping with amusement. One of my EPA friends, ignoring the jibe, threw his own challenge right back. "If you can figure an acceptable way to advertise that special feature," he joshed, "Concorde will never want for lady customers."

On a preschedule one-day trial run from Boston to Paris and back, Concorde's French representative invited me (meaning EPA) to come and judge the Concorde for myself. For a moment I felt the tug of temptation—to eat breakfast and supper in Boston with a leisurely Parisian lunch in between. Then I could visualize the headline: "EPA OFFICIAL SIPS IN-FLIGHT CHAMPAGNE AS HE PONDERS FATE OF CONCORDE." I declined.

A few months later Transportation Secretary William T. Coleman, Jr., gave his judicious ruling: Try the half dozen or so Concordes already in existence for sixteen months of service between Europe and Dulles Airport. That would allow our federal technicians time to measure whatever hurt and hazard Concorde might carry along with its startling speed.

Now, back to the ozone matter. Paul Crutzen claimed that the input of nitric oxide into the ozone area due to nuclear testing prior to 1963 equaled the effect of several hundred SSTs.[5] This means that any observed variations in total ozone may have taken place strictly from open-air explosions of nuclear weapons. If so, we have another good reason to decry the deliberate continuance of these experiments by the Chinese and the French, in defiance of United Nations coaxing to join the United States-USSR test ban.

The ozone enemy we have heard most about is fluorocarbons. These inert gases propel spray out of cans of deodorants, hair control liquids, shaving creams, and the like, and also serve as the coolant in refrigerators. Also known as halocarbon, chlorofluoromethane, Freon (by Dupont), or the Russian trade name of Eskimon, fluorocarbons have squirted their way into households on every continent. In 1974 scientists Rowland and Molina made a frightening pronouncement: Fluorocarbons decompose into chlorines and other compounds when they reach ultraviolet rays in the stratosphere. This is bad because the chlorine in turn breaks down ozone, they said.

This news panicked consumers and manufacturers alike. Ecology-minded users of spray cans wanted to give them up immediately. Executives of the $10-million industry mostly wailed "Wait a minute!" To begin with both were right: the eco-freaks because, if you don't have to take a risk, why take it, the industry spokesmen because freon aerosols aren't the only cause for shrinkage of the ozone layer. For one thing, the depth of the ozone layer normally differs from place to place over the globe: It might be thick over Grand Rapids, Michigan, and thin over Plains, Georgia. But the differences are constantly in flux.

The country was in a quandary. More information was needed before the responsible people in government and business could make the decision—to regulate fluorocarbons or not.

At last the National Academy of Sciences broke the logjam in 1976, with its long-awaited judgment of whether fluorocarbons really are ripping off the ozone zone.[6] Their answer (heavily hedged with scientific qualifications) is yes—though the time frame is long. There will be a two-fold result, they declare: Not only will more ultraviolet rays penetrate the air at the earth's surface and endanger all flora and fauna, but disruption of the ozone layer will also let in more infrared rays, which will build up atmospheric heat and affect the earth's climate.

There will also be another effect, I believe, though it is not mentioned in the Academy's report. As the aerosols—or fine particles of the fluorocarbons—collect in the stratosphere like smoke in a crowded barroom, they most likely will interrupt the passage of sunlight to the earth. Since solar energy is the atmosphere's prime mover, this condition is also apt to influence weather and climate.

Additional surprises stud the Academy's statement, drawn up by its Committee on Impacts of Stratospheric Change: For example, if we continue to release fluorocarbons at the same rate we did in 1973, they will some years from now remove 7 percent of the ozone layer.

Therefore, says the report, "In our present state of knowledge it would be imprudent to accept increasing use and release, [of fluorocarbons], either in the United States or worldwide."

However, the report shows that the interchange between ozone and fluorocarbons takes place very slowly. For instance, even if we banned fluorocarbons right now, as we may do, ozone would nevertheless continue to be depleted for at least a decade by the fluorocarbons already released up to now. Then ozone reduction would almost imperceptibly taper off at roughly one seventieth of its current value each year, not reaching zero for a hundred years. In other words, fluorocarbons' present destructiveness of the ozone layer will go on, though at a diminishing rate, for a century.

So fluorocarbons will not kill or maim anybody, nor will they ruin our climate tomorrow. Furthermore, the Academy is confident that even if more disquieting facts emerge and we have to stop using fluorocarbons, it will be safe enough to wait another year or two before doing so.

Nevertheless, EPA acted quickly in response to the report. EPA Administrator Russell E. Train told his research team to initiate the scientific investigation necessary to establish regulations as soon as possible. Train also urged our NATO allies and the Soviets, who with the United States and Japan are the major makers and users of fluorocarbons, to begin similar studies. Train then invited environmental leaders of eleven of these countries to meet in Washington in April 1977 to determine whether international regulation should be imposed. This followed a UN meeting on fluorocarbons the preceding month.

Train asked the Food and Drug Administration (FDA) to participate in the April conclave because 80 percent of the spray products (hair spray, deodorants, shaving cream, and the like) rank as cosmetics and fit into FDA's regulatory domain. Out of these two meetings came a consensus that the flurocarbons do constitute a serious problem and that accelerated study of the threat they pose must be done before corrective action can be determined.

Apparently there are numerous other dynamic systems in the atmosphere which may be affecting the ozone curtain. But the Academy's findings—plus the fact that we have 10,000 additional cases of skin cancer each year, synchronized with annual increases in the sale of fluorocarbons—give our government no excuse for standing still.

Train first raised the idea of international regulation among our NATO allies back in 1975. Characteristically, he was moving while others were waiting to be told. Now that Train's courage and foresight have been justified by the Academy study, serious thinking must begin on how to regulate. Regulation will have to be selective, since some of the uses of fluorocarbon are frivolous and others are more essential. About 85 percent of the fluorocarbons that are leaking upward come from spray cans; and most of the rest come from worn-out freezers and air conditioners, which must use a dependable refrigerant such as Freon. About half the total quantity of fluorocarbons released globally every year has been from the United States. When regulation commences, cosmetics—representing some 68 percent of all fluorocarbon releases—must be the first to go, and American consumers and producers will have to give up more of these dubious products than anyone else. The other 17 percent of spray cans carry such products as paint, pesticides, and medicines, which can all be sprayed mechanically rather than by using the now dreaded fluorocarbons. Furthermore, the irrepressible inventor of the original spray cans, Robert Abplanalp has already patented a nonflammable substitute for fluorocarbons: It is a mixture of natural gas and water. This is nonpoisonous, and when it does get into the atmosphere it just breaks down as if burned, producing carbon dioxide and water.

Not all climate-threatening pollutants will be as simple to draw a bead on as the fluorocarbons. Yet some of them carry a more immediate and obvious threat, especially sky dust, heat, and carbon dioxide (CO_2).

SKY DUST

The day in 1971 that fixed sky dust in my memory began as I was awakened in the early morning blackness by two gentle finger taps on the windowpane. It was my thoughtful traveling companion, Dr. Lester Machta, a NOAA meteorologist. He was trying not to rouse me at six A.M. as he peeled an adhesive strip off the window. He had stuck it there before bedtime to measure the quantity of dust in the air over Alma Ata, Kazakhstan. He and I were touring the Soviet Union as air pollution specialists on an exchange visit. Dr. Machta is so keen on research that, like Vincent Schaefer, he monitors air quality wherever he is.

He has concentrated for years on gathering knowledge about inadvertent man-made hurts to the environment, such as the scattering of dust in the air.

Human activity releases a tremendous amount of dust into the atmosphere. Cement factories, cities, poorly tended farms, and dirt roads head the list. Yet estimates indicate that anthropogenic (man's) contribution is only 1 to 5 percent of the total, which emanates mostly from volcanoes and deserts. Sulfur dioxide adds to the total when it is converted into sulfates, which are particulates (dust). Hence, control of sulfates is important for climate protection as well as for health. Sulfates from factories, power plants, and motor vehicles warm the lower atmosphere, as all dust does. This statement sounds peculiar because one might expect that dust gathering into dry clouds would reflect the sun's rays away from the earth and cooling would ensure—and it does. But here we run into one of those intellectual traffic jams in which scientists can't agree with each other. One group, relying on a computer model, concludes that the dust cover not only bounces solar heat back into the sky, but also prevents heat generated on the earth from escaping. This group says, furthermore, that the dust entraps more heat under it in the atmosphere than it reflects away above it.

Professor Reid Bryson, whom I saw in his office at the University of Wisconsin, is a meteorologist on the other side of the fence. I had anticipated going to Madison not only to see this well-known expert, but also to escape from a nasty air pollution alert in Washington. Dr. Bryson lived up to my expectations. But the air over this once pristine country town was acrid from the combustion of high sulfur coal in the power plant, which had been designed to use natural gas—before the shortage.

Dr. Bryson speaks softly, but feels strong convictions on climate: He says flatly that the dust will reduce incoming sunlight and will cool the earth. As a matter of fact he is greatly exercised by the terrifying totals of dust that are now rising, forming a really dense cover. He's not talking, as most scientists do, about the industrial sources of dust. He's pointing his finger at the slash-and-burn agricultural practices in the unurbanized places like Laos, Brazil, and Zaire, which Bryson claims are dumping 60 million tons of dust and smoke particles into the atmosphere every year. He believes these will accumulate up near the stratosphere and will screen out substantial amounts of solar energy.

The resultant drop in temperature in the northern hemisphere, Bryson fears, will lead to lessening productivity of the soil. Then the United States and Canada, which produce and distribute some 70 percent of the world's grain supply, will be unable to keep up their present volume. Soon food shortages will occur which will lead to trouble between the have and have-not nations. As mentioned in chapter 3, Professor Budyko in the Soviet Union holds the opposite view: that the earth is warming and harvests will be improving, not worsening.

Since Bryson and his fellow thinker at Boulder's National Center for Atmospheric Research, Stephen Schneider, are convinced that cooling is taking place, they have been pleading publicly in their speeches and writings that the government start planning remedies. Schneider's book *The Genesis Strategy* [7] likens the situation to that of biblical times, when there were alternate periods of famine and prosperity and it was necessary to plan during good times for upcoming stretches of privation.

I heard Schneider talk eloquently in this vein before the Senate Foreign Relations Committee. The Congress, the White House, and other centers of leadership in this country are still biding their time before acting: They want to hear all the pleaders; but these are so many and so various that it will be some years, I think, before any sort of political consensus arises.

Meanwhile, dust also has an important impact on precipitation. Every snowflake, every raindrop, every fog molecule forms around a nucleus, a particle. Yet here we run into more of the sort of contradiction that so often frustrates scientists' ability to comprehend what's happening up there in the clouds. Wilmot Hess's classic compendium *Weather and Climate Modification* [8] discusses this one thoroughly, as it does many other questions of physical meteorology that baffle us nontechnical observers. Hess's book includes an article by Lester Machta and Kosta Telegadis [9] that reveals two clear facts about dust nuclei and precipitation:

One is that there are already more cloud condensation nuclei floating around in the sky than are needed to squeeze rain out of all existing clouds. (Since clouds regularly obscure more than half of the globe, that is a stupendous quantity of dust.) The other point is that an excess of nuclei may actually decrease precipitation. I shall skip a blow-by-blow argument in favor of the latter view because even the experts disagree on why this is so.

But dust does affect rainfall—both triggers it and inhibits it. Whether or not we accept Reid Bryson's conclusion as to what 60 million tons of dust are doing to the climate the world community should start thinking about how to reduce that almost incomprehensible weight of atmospheric dirt. In our country the 1970 Clean Air Act amendments call for limits on particulate matter, or dust. But EPA, which administers the law, bases its criteria on what dust does to human health, and pays no attention to the impact on climate. So to get at the problem will require executive action or new legislation—even in the United States, where in general the antipollution machinery is more effective than anywhere else.

HEAT

As I write this from my Georgetown, D.C., study, in the wicked winter of 1977 I have on three sweaters and the President is asking us to turn down our thermostats. It does seem a paradox that in the midst of an endless cold snap and a world fuel shortage a major environmental issue is the alleged rise in the level of heat in the atmosphere. Along with Professor Budyko of the USSR, the United States Navy's Dr. Howard A. Wilcox said the rise is real, in his 1975 book *Hothouse Earth*.[10] A generally accepted figure right now is that if you compare man-made heat with solar heat globally, the ratio is only in the range of 1:100 to 1:1,000, but in any given city the ratio ranges from 1:10 to 1:1. Dr. Wilcox says bluntly that the global proportion will accelerate rapidly if we continue to increase consumption of fossil fuels at the present rate of 4 to 6 percent per year. He proclaims that "almost certainly within eighty to one hundred eighty years from now—the ice caps will quickly melt".[11]

Wilcox says that despite the warnings about inadequate fuel supplies we have enough oil, coal, gas, uranium, and (in the oceans) hydrogen to serve our civilization for hundreds of years. He says we can anticipate a 5 percent growth rate in thermal pollution annually for an indefinite period; but this would soon bring the earth to temperatures unacceptable for people, animals, and crops.

Just after he returned from an official inspection of the navy base at McMurdo Sound in the Antarctic this winter, I encountered J. William Middendorf, the Secretary of the Navy. Since Wilcox worked for the navy, I asked the secretary whether he seriously believed the globe is getting hotter to the degree described by Wilcox. Middendorf replied, "Well, I know about the curves these scientists draw and I know that Wilcox is a first-class oceanographer. However, after flying over two thousand miles of solid ice to the South Pole I can't really accept that prognostication."

Middendorf had visited the bases of Britain's Captain Robert Scott, who died just after reaching the Pole in 1912. He was fascinated with the base at Cape Evans, which has remained so untouched by time that two of Scott's frozen dogs and a portion of seal meat still lie nearby. Biscuits left on the table in the building where expedition members lived are as fresh today as when Scott departed on his tragic last journey. Middendorf had tasted one two days before I saw him and conceded it was quite eatable.

The tall secretary, his face still glowing from the crisp polar cold, clearly found "Hothouse Earth" a hard concept to swallow.

But the *Study of Man's Impact on Climate* (with its awful acronym SMIC)[12] comes down on nearly the same ground as Wilcox. They forecast a possible rise *or* fall in the average planetary temperature of about 1°F, due to the impurities poured by man into the atmosphere. According to some respectable scientists, a tiny 1°F rise will melt the ice caps, and a 1°F drop will start a new Ice Age. As simple as that.

So far, the major direct input of heat from our civilization into the atmosphere comes from burning fossil fuels and from the cooling towers of nuclear plants. We also drive up the global thermometer indirectly by unloading carbon dioxide into the air, again mostly through the combustion of fossil fuels.

CARBON DIOXIDE (CO_2)

Since the beginning of industrialization, the quantity of CO_2 in the atmosphere has risen about 10 percent. What is more extraordinary is that approximately 50 percent of all the CO_2 emitted by fossil fuels from 1860 to 1970 has remained airborne. In the past, volcanoes produced most of the CO_2 in the sky; but fossil fuels are now delivering a load a hundred times as great as that from volcanoes. Another source of CO_2 compares with fossil fuels in the volume of CO_2 produced: This is the turning of natural pastures and woods into cultivated croplands, cutting down on the amount of natural humus in the soil; the new crops emit more CO_2 than humus does.

Dr. Machta, director of NOAA's air resources lab, calls carbon dioxide "the atmospheric constituent most often mentioned in expressing concern that man may be altering the climate."

Listening to other climatologists lends credence to Dr. Machta's view, I have learned, even though some observers think there are other dangers much more critical than the buildup of CO_2. For example, chemical reactions to industry's effluvia might end in our involuntarily depleting our oxygen supply to the point at which it could no longer support life. Or the reactions might go the other way and stimulate the formation of more oxygen: If the quantity of oxygen in the air envelope around us should jump from its present 21 percent to 25 percent, all the forests and combustible man-made structures on the earth would automatically kindle and burn.[13] These fantasies are not likely to become real, says Dr. Machta, but they could.

Well, what's so bad about CO_2? Why should we try to shut back its growing preponderance in the atmosphere? Because scientists like Howard Wilcox are convinced that it prevents heat from escaping the atmosphere, so that the heat radiates back and forth inside, like the air in a greenhouse with the windows shut. When this process goes on long enough, the average temperature of air and ocean will increase and thaw the polar ice caps (known as the cryosphere) and the glaciers. The consequent melting of millions of tons of ice and snow would elevate the global sea some 100 meters and bury all seaports and populated coastal zones underwater. Lester Machta has provided a schematic map (figure 6) which delineates the new high tide marks in the aftermath of the melting.

Such an event would not happen as rapidly as a tidal wave, of course, but slowly—over decades, at the fastest. Looking at the bright side, one has to admit that it would force rather large-scale urban renewal! This is not just an idle thought, for the thousands of square miles of habitable shorelines that would be lost to flooding would be replaced by a fairly equivalent area of new, virgin land formerly covered by ice sheets, Another dream of Jules Verne would come true—that envisaged in the *Purchase of the North Pole*[14]—although the means of its realization would be somewhat different than from Verne's—which was to switch the earth's axis.

But Lester Machta's view of such forecasts is, "Not so fast!"

What he foresees is that although CO_2 will indeed increase and warm the atmosphere, the consequences aren't nearly so black-and-white as worriers of the Wilcox type envision them.

Dr. Machta derives his figures and deductions from a mathematical model by S. Manabe. According to this model the present concentration of CO_2 is about 320 parts per million "ppm" throughout the total atmosphere. With 385 ppm expected, by the year 2000 (at the current rate of increase), the lower part of the atmosphere will have become 0.5°C warmer, says the model.[15]

This situation could affect the climate in two ways, explains Machta. First, the warmer air could speed up the rate of evaporation from the sea and from land water, and more clouds would appear; and the additional cloud cover would cut the quantity of incoming solar heat, thus *cooling* the lower atmosphere. On the other hand, a hotter lower atmosphere would probably warm the sea's surface, which when warmer gives up more CO_2; and with more CO_2 the air would be warmer and the puzzling cycle would "grow by what it feeds upon," as Shakespeare said, or get "positive feedback" as today's scientists put it—or the faster we run, the farther behind we get, as we learned from Alice in *Through the Looking Glass*. The atmosphere simply won't stay still long enough for us to focus on its secrets.

But then, as the reader has doubtless noticed in recent press accounts, accurate meteorological monitoring reveals that the earth has chilled infinitesimally, about 0.5°C since 1940. Doomsayers like Lowell Ponte, author of *The Cooling*,[16] extrapolate from this

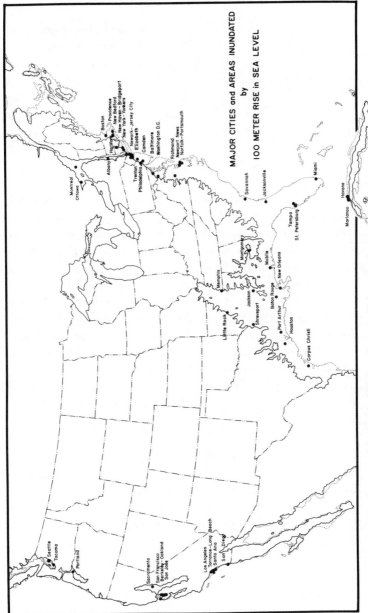

Fig. 6. Major cities and areas of the United States that would be inundated by a 100-meter rise in sea level.

fact that ice caps are silently sliding southwards; circumpolar vortex (the constant winds around the North Pole) is reaching farther south; the jet stream is switching its direction; the monsoons and hurricanes are being pushed off their course and thus are upsetting expected rain patterns; and we are careening smack at a new Ice Age, preceded by terrible droughts. Reid Bryson's report that enormous swirls of anthropogenic dust will contribute to a cooling of the planet adds credibility to the Ice Age forecast, and reminds us that if an Ice Age does come, mankind may well have produced it.

In order to keep our bearings through all this confusion, it is helpful to remember Michael MacCracken's view that climate's "norm" is ultimately going to prove abnormal. It's a shame that he wasn't on hand to comfort our forbears during the strange summer of 1816, when summer never did come to New England. Instead of heat waves and sunburn and summer squalls, all the Down Easters saw that June, July, and August were sleet storms, chilblains, and blizzards! It is mind-boggling to imagine what today's computer-rich scientists would deduce from that experience, when they ring the disaster bell at a mere 0.5°C switch in thirty-odd years. One explanation is that 1816's wintry summer followed the eruption of Krakatoa, which tossed up several cubic miles of smoke and ash that circled the globe and thus held back solar rays for almost three years.

To finish our summary of CO_2 loads in the atmosphere: Man is producing more than six billion tons of CO_2 every year and only a fraction of it is absorbed by the oceans, plus another small amount by the trees and green plants. This vast input warms the climate in local areas, but the dust burden cuts out sunlight, cooling the climate overall. Which of these two effects will predominate? We don't know yet.

CONTRAILS

A special suspect as a climatic villan is the high, fleecy cirrus left in the wake of an airplane flying above 30,000 feet. It's known as a contrail. This plane-made cloud forms when water vapor in the jet's exhaust condenses into gossamer traces of ice. Would-be guardians of our climate claim that contrails reflect solar energy away from the earth and therefore add to the cooling effects of dust.

It may be that these warners are right, but so far their proofs are unconvincing. One fact they cite is that the sunshine meter, a handy little gadget invented by meteorologists in the late 1950s, already registers a slight lowering in the quantity of sunlight reaching the earth. They argue that this is happening because contrails intercept the incoming solar rays. So far this conclusion seems speculative.

ALBEDO

Another accusation is that human activities such as deforestation and urbanization have changed the earth's albedo: the ability of the planet to reflect away the sun's beams—its mirror quality, so to speak. The more solar radiation our planet reflects back into space, the less energy we receive from the sun.

Figure 7 sets forth the comparative albedos of various sorts of surfaces.[17] It is clear that concrete, sand, and even dark soils and areas covered by green growth reflect less light and heat when they are wet than when they are dry. The figure shows unequivocally that snow, ice, and clouds are the most efficient reflectors. In short, even man's most egregious misuse of land causes the loss of less energy through albedo than is lost by these natural surfaces. Deforestation, urbanization, and desertification—the spreading of deserts—gravely damage other aspects of the environment, but the changes they inflict on albedo are, so far, comparatively insignificant.

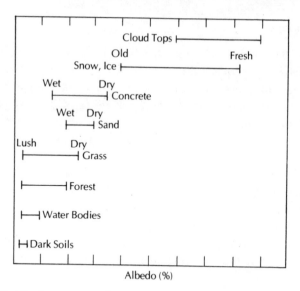

Fig. 7. Albedo—percent of reflectivity—for various surfaces (after Slade). (From Wilmot N. Hess, ed., *Weather and Climate Modification*)

MARINE POLLUTION

Oil slicks constantly besmirch the ocean, mainly from ships running aground, colliding, or cleaning their bilges and lately from offshore drilling blowouts. Estuaries also pass along to the ocean oily evidence of a myriad sloppy fuel handlers upstream. Jacques Cousteau keeps telling us these slicks are extending themselves over ever wider stretches and may well change the albedo of the seven seas. If so, there will be effects as yet unknown—but probably bad, according to numerous climatologists.

Cousteau says the sickness of the seas is spreading and heading to a terrible finale. In painful detail, he dramatizes the inevitable day when the smothering oil, with traces of heavy metals and other pollutants, will totally wipe out all marine organisms, including the precious phytoplankton, the omnipresent base of the food triangle in the global ocean. When the phytoplankton go, says Cousteau, we will lose a prime producer of oxygen, in the sea; and without adequate oxygen to dilute and purify the air at sea level, pollutants will overwhelm the sea-level atmosphere. Two thirds of mankind will perish, and the surviving third will crawl gasping up into the hills for the remaining breathable air.

Cousteau may be more a persuasive salesman than a scientist; he does seem to project such terroristic scenes beyond the data available to support them. However, the cause of ecology certainly benefits when he stirs up public sentiment against uncontrolled pollution of the sea. Furthermore, even if he can't yet prove that what he fears will actually come to pass, who has enough facts to disprove him?

NUCLEAR POWER PLANTS

Nuclear power plants may help to upset the planetary heat balance, as we have seen. They may also carry another concealed threat to natural weather patterns—the noble gas krypton. If nuclear power plants continue to multiply for a hundred years, the release of krypton has the potential to make a lot of mischief with the weather. Here's how: Krypton is released in significant quantities during the reprocessing of nuclear fuel. Nature's only way of disposing of accumulations of this gas is radioactive decay. As this occurs, the gas ionizes and thus affects the electrical properties of the atmosphere around it. "This problem of the future could affect thunderstorm activity and associated precipitation patterns," is what scientist W. L. Boeck—supported by Bernard Vonnegut, of early cloud-seeding note, and others—predict.[18]

In short, krypton decay may scramble the whole system of moisture interchange between oceans and atmosphere. Such interference could provoke droughts or floods in regions where power plants are located. This prophesy of peril warrants careful research; nuclear expansion should not go ahead without our knowing the true facts about this threat.

As we begin to track all these man-made thrusts at climate and understand what catastrophes they may bring if not stopped, scientists at Livermore Laboratory, at NOAA, and elsewhere leave us with the haunting question: At what point will man's influence on climate become irreversible, like the effects of Dr. Jekyll's evil potion?

CITIES TODAY

Studies have already given us clues as to what the combination of urbanization and industrialization in one city mean to the weather of the city and of the countryside downwind of it. These studies concentrated on Saint Louis, Missouri. To get an overall idea of what they show, think of the city as a pile of rocks on a riverbed and the prevailing wind mass moving like a river overhead. The turbulence in the current of wind when it hits the city bears a remarkable resemblance to that in the rapids where a river hits a rocky bottom.

If you stand on the banks of the Congo River at Brazzaville you can see this turbulence (as I did), in a natural spectacle of extraordinary violence. The river, flowing at the awesome rate of millions of gallons per second, was leaping up into a solid wall of white water higher than a two story house, and dwarfed me on the ground alongside. Yet only a hundred yards or so upstream the surface was smooth and unrippled. What was causing this wild, tumbling turmoil? What was the mechanism of this monster Waring blender, which ground up the Congo's ubiquitous water lillies so fine that the river downstream turned to an even, avocado green? The river was simply passing over a bed studded with great rocky protuberances.

A similar turbulence occurs in the air when a breeze blowing steadily across a flat rural landscape collides with the bulky sharp-cornered buildings of a modern city. Over Saint Louis the air is tossed some 2,000 feet upwards. That's not all the city does to that peaceful, unsuspecting wind gliding over the Missouri prairie. St. Louis throws in most of the irritants we've been talking about—

heat, carbon dioxide, dust, Freons, and other pollutants—to make a filthy potpourri of urban offal. Any suffering denizen of a city knows what's in the air; if not, he has only to look skyward, and he will soon need to blink. What we want to know here is whether these ingredients are changing the weather and the climate. They are. In fact, the unintended impact of cities is the most measurable, so far, of all the anthropogenic activities that affect climate or weather.

First, there is the ceaseless radiation of heat—not only from combustion (in autos, power plants and cooling towers, factories, furnaces, and air conditioners) but also from the albedo of the city's concrete and stone and windows, all bouncing back the sun's rays. Thousands of heat freshets of all sizes and intensities combine into one gigantic wave over the city. Meterologists describe this as the city plume, or "heat Island," in the passing sea of the atmosphere. Into this towering, invisible contour the city also pumps moisture from auto exhausts, steam from powerplants, and evaporation from rivers, lakes, reservoirs, and water treatment works. Also into this mixture (as we've mentioned) go all kinds of particulate matter which provides nuclei for cloud condensation, often perfect for rainmaking.

All these factors have been measured in an experiment called "Metromex," another silly-sounding acronym which means Metropolitan Meterological Experiment. It was conducted in 1971 by Stanley Changnon, leading a team of scientists from various universities and government laboratories. After Saint Louis, Changnon studied another seven cities as well—Chicago, Indianapolis, Cleveland, Washington, Houston, New Orleans, and Tulsa—to check for unintended effects modifying precipitation.

Changnon and his teams found that the most pronounced effect of cities on rainfall occurs when there is already moderate to heavy rain. The urban presence serves as a rain stimulant to existing rain clouds. For would-be weather modifiers this implies that we have discovered a new, dependable means to render an ongoing rain process more efficient by seeding.

Another way to look at it is that the urban heat island, by which the grimy dusts of the city are lifted into the clouds, operates like the ground generators used by commercial cloud seeders. In Metromex the increase in precipitation increase was found to be proportional to the size of the city, the kind of industrial nuclei produced, the volume and temperature of the city heat plume, and the amount of moisture added by industrial sources such as cooling towers. Metromex and other studies reveal that these urban phenomena increase rain, cloud coverage, and the severity of local storms.

We now know also that the man-made dust particles dancing above a city may lead to light rain or snow when no precipitation is expected by the weatherman. New Yorkers frequently see this happen.

The most significant and potentially devastating imprint of a city on weather quality is what happens downwind. By contrasting weather in the lee of large cities with upwind weather, Metromex recorded more rain volume and more intense storms forty miles downwind of the city than upwind.

To sum up, urban complexes, especially if they are heavily industrialized, bring increases in atmospheric contaminants such as particulate matter, gaseous mixtures, and carbon dioxide as well as cloud cover, fog, rain, snow, and higher temperatures. Cities also decrease or disrupt wind speed, increase relative humidity, and decrease the incidence of sunshine and untraviolet radiation.

What's that? Isn't it *healthful* to reduce ultraviolet rays? Not totally, say Dr. James T. Peterson and Edwin C. Flowers, both NOAA meteorologists assigned to EPA's lab in Durham, North Carolina. They explain that ultraviolet radiation comprises a small, but chemically and biologically important proportion of total solar radiation. It provides vitamin D in the human body, and is responsible for tanning. But here is the bad news: It is also a prime factor in forming photochemical smog. On the other hand, there's some good in smog: It disrupts ultraviolet radiation on its path to sunbathers and everyone else, removing as much as 35 percent of the ultraviolet in the smog capital of Los Angeles, and 6 percent or 7 percent in a city like Saint Louis. The balance between the good and the bad of UV is a delicate one.

A final note on what cities and factories do to climate. The effects downwind of Saint Louis as borne out in Metromex show that cities degrade climate, but we have found no patterns as yet as to how far the downwind effects travel, nor how severe they are, nor how long they last nor what sort of quirky weather may ensue. Second, because of its dangers the city becomes a potential enemy of other cities or regions of its own country, not to mention the nations downwind. These problems will be discussed in chapter 8.

Meanwhile, urbanized, industrialized human settlement provides a ready-made laboratory for weather and climate research that may yield up secrets even the smartest computers can't fathom: Having begun to discover specific cause-and-effect principles between the city plume and the local and downwind climate we will be in a constantly improving position to forecast local and regional weather, and be better able to modify weather as we wish.

If one city disrupts and deteriorates the weather, think what a megalopolis may accomplish. This hideous new entity of civilization—cities mestastasizing until they engulf a whole region—is already a reality in the northeast corridor of the United States, from Washington to Boston. With one city a climatic hazard, will a megalopolis of ten cities be worse by a factor of ten or a hundred, or what?

Unintended human damage to climate, weather, and environment is a bit like the depredations of a wild animal that has broken out of the zoo. Our civilization is threatened by it. Meanwhile the responsible environmental departments of government are in the predicament of the blind pigmy trying to identify an elephant by touch: They have still much to learn before they can even describe the animal accurately; and they will have to describe it accurately in order to protect us from it.

PART THREE

Environmental Modification: Future

7

COUNTERATTACK ON
UNINTENDED ECOCIDE

Man has been soiling his surroundings thoughtlessly. He has become a sort of ecological bed wetter. To environment-train him is an idea whose time has been forced to come. Four forces pushed it: Rachel Carson, the Swedes, American ecology groups, and Maurice Strong of the United Nations. Jointly they laid the foundation for an international mission to rescue our suffering life-support systems. All nations owe this emergency squad gratitude for telling us to slow down before we smash forever the delicate biological and climatic mechanism called the biosphere. Above all we must build on what they've done.

Why and how did they do it? No one was going to make any money out of such an issue, no territory was going to change hands, no great personal power or popularity would accrue to the heroes of this movement. Indeed, William D. Ruckelshaus, the brilliant first head of the United States Environmental Protection Agency (EPA), was introduced to a large meeting of manufacturers as the "greatest friend of American business since Karl Marx." This was said in jest, but the laughter it drew didn't totally dilute the sting behind the joke.

They did it by using their talent and energy unselfishly to appeal to the enlightened self-interest of citizens of this earth.

Their campaign grew out of their convictions. It picked up momentum as its logic was communicated from one person to another, and then from one nation to another, until the crescendo in the great conclave staged by the United Nations in Stockholm in 1972.

What's Past Is Prologue

The environmentalists of this decade have organized a counterattack on unintended man-made messes in our environment, weather, and climate. This chapter will examine the national, bilateral, and multilateral arrangements that I hope will comprise the basis of a future planetary protection system.

Rachel Carson's stirring 1963 book on the ravages of pesticides, *Silent Spring*,[1] started the ball rolling in the United States. *Silent Spring* depicts the stilling of birds and the insects they once thrived on, now dead from pesticidal overkill.

Silent Spring became an instant best seller. Its readers began talking and writing and forming citizen action clubs. By the end of the 1960s, a total of some 300 private save-the-environment groups had sprung up around the nation. They oversimplified their pitch to dramatize it: "This threat is worse than anything else you can think of except nuclear warfare; unless we act soon, mankind will die as a goldfish does when nobody changes his fouled water."

Millions of Americans agreed; and soon a silent but loyal constituency stood behind the activists—silent except as measured by opinion polls and (in the 1970s) at the polls. In the 1974 congressional campaign, twelve antienvironment incumbents were tagged the "Dirty Dozen." All but four lost in the elections.

Sweden, in the van of social betterment, as usual, formed the first environmental protection agency in 1967. Next year Sweden proposed a United Nations meeting to alert all peoples on the eco-crisis. The United Nations General Assembly of 1969 voted to hold the conference. Then in 1970, Maurice Strong of Canada stepped up to bat as secretary general of the "United Nations Conference on the Human Environment," the formal title of the meeting.

The mustachioed, mild-mannered Mr. Strong was an inspired choice. This genial, earnest millionaire industrialist, had served as a youthful summer intern at the United Nations Secretariat headquarters in New York. From his teens he had been imbued with the ideals and goals of the United Nations. As a manufacturer, he had seen firsthand the ravages from uncontrolled exploitation of natural resources. His United Nations selectors saw how powerfully motivated he might be. They were right. Almost from the day of his appointment Mr. Strong plunged into his task with merry but messianic fervor. Strong faced a long stormy voyage, for world interest in the environment was spotty.

The developing nations hadn't heard much, if anything, about the flurry of eco-worry that Rachel Carson and the American lobbying groups had generated. In the United States, Congress passed a new Clean Air Act; and the administration established the EPA, in response to the public clamor to *do* something.

The movement was also under way in Europe, with the British Department of the Environment following Sweden into a national program and with France and Germany and the Soviet Union taking mini-steps toward regulating pollution.

So Mr. Strong's four preparatory meetings in New York and Geneva were supported by the United States and European nations, as well as Canada, Mexico, Brazil, India, and Japan. But this handful of nations—mostly industrialized nations—wasn't enough for the meeting to gain its goal: to get all the world to start corrective action.

Maurice Strong saw what had to be done and did it. He headed for the regional centers of Asia, the Far East, Africa, and South

America, and with almost Christ-like patience and salesmanship, brought along the ignorant, the doubting, the suspicious, and even the hostile political nabobs. For almost two years he traveled endlessly, visited scores of countries, and met every objection with friendly, informed argument. When the conference finally convened in the warm June sunshine of Stockholm in 1972, Strong had a total of 113 national delegations, comprising over a thousand conferees, in camp.

The only notable no-shows were the Soviets. They stayed away because of a dispute over the admission of East Germany, but they had worked hard and helpfully in the preparatory sessions. A nonsmoker, I remember sitting between the Soviet and American chief delegates at one of the sessions—the Soviet being a chain cigar burner and the American, a nonstop pipe puffer. The fumes were so thick I couldn't see Maurice Strong on the platform. That discomfort etched sharply in my mind one fact of life that hinders the eco-movement: Pollution abatement is good medicine for the *other* fellow.

Several hundred "camp followers" also arrived in Stockholm. These were largely the private American ecology groups, plus similar groups from a few other countries. We bureaucrats call them "NGOs"—nongovernmental organizations. NGOs of all types follow the United Nations operations in New York. In fact, they frequently use the United Nations premises for important meetings. The Swedes lent them a headquarters about a mile away from the official convention site. The NGOs had a full agenda which proceeded simultaneously with the official one.

There is a geographical peculiarity about Stockholm in June—one which may have heightened the tensions that grew up in the two weeks ahead. I noticed it my first night there. My bedtime book was less soporific than I expected, so I finished it and turned off the light—but the room was still light. The sun had quietly risen at two A.M. With so few hours of darkness, the whole city was sleeping less. This meant that the hardworking conferees would be going more and more on nervous energy—and hence more apt to be sharp in interpersonal dealings.

A Politicized Conference

Besides, the conference was heavily politicized. Like the Olympics, the environment is essentially a nonpolitical issue. But some tend to use such events as the conference or the Olympics as forums to advance unrelated ideas. At Stockholm the Chinese People's Republic vilified the United States with charges of imperialism; and the then Swedish Prime Minister Palme accused the Americans of committing ecocide in Vietnam. This sentiment had been running high even before the meeting: Many of our embassy's windows were still broken when we arrived, despite the popularity of our ambassador, Jerome H. Holland.

Additionally the NGO meeting became at times a hotbed of anti-American activity on the Vietnam issue. At least one leading United States ecologist committed what seemed to me a despicable act: He denounced his country before a foreign audience. Hoping to achieve a better balance of thought over there, Bill Ruckelshaus bravely agreed to address the NGOs one night. A few of us accompanied him—closely, as we weren't totally confident of his security in such an atmosphere. We had one touchy moment when an obviously handicapped Japanese (perhaps with mercury poisoning) lurched toward Ruckelshaus on the speaker's stand with a suspicious-looking paper bag in his hands. Two of us gently but quickly intercepted him.

The rowdy event ended happily. Ruckelshaus's candor, healthy humor, and knowledge converted the antagonism of most of the 500 listeners to cheers and applause.

Other political activity included efforts by two or three Latin American countries to increase their influence in the Third World. Since these maneuverers were also working hard for the conference, their activity seemed all to the good. One colorful demonstration against whale slaughter captured citywide attention, with a fifty-foot-long, black papier-maché model of a whale circulating through the streets.

Of course some of the poorer nations tried to use the conference as a lever to pry development funds out of the rich ones. There had also been an undercurrent of talk for a year or more that the conference was a sneaky plot by the industrialized nations: "They want to impose environment controls on us poorer countries to shackle our efforts to grow and compete with them economically," was the allegation.

World Bank president Robert McNamara merits our gratitude for persuading the Third World representatives that there was no such plot. He said in his speech that the bank had for some time required loans for capital projects to be contingent on being constructed in a way that would not harm the environment. He explained that the bank had computed the difference in cost between projects that are environmentally sound and those that are not, and found it to be negligible.

We of the United States delegation were advancing a corollary concept in corridor conversations: It is far cheaper to industralize with environmental controls built in as an integral part of the system than to have to retrofit them later. We explained that America has to spring-clean the oldest industrial complex in the world: Because of the bombing in World War II the Europeans have a far higher percentage of new plants than our country, which has never been bombed. EPA's original estimate of what it would cost the United States to implement the first ten years of its new antipollution legislation was $187 billion.

The American delegation numbered over sixty, from the government and from the private sectors. Russell E. Train, then Chairman of the President's Environmental Council, headed this huge group. Two standout members were the EPA chief, William D. Ruckelshaus, and Senator Howard Baker, shortly to become a national TV personality in the Senate hearings on Watergate. Senator Claiborne Pell also attended. He chairs the Senate Foreign Relations Committee's subcommittee on oceans and the environment. John Ehrlichman, briefly present, said he liked my suggestion of a bilateral agreement with the Chinese and would support it at the White House. But he left suddenly in mid-conference, perhaps because Watergate started to unreel at just that moment.

The delegation fought firmly to quell the efforts of others to turn the conference into a political quagmire. We beseeched our fellow participants to concentrate on the environment, something we all could agree on regardless of political creed or committment. This approach touched the right note. It finally typified the attitude of almost all delegations.

Shirley Temple Black of our delegation played a unique role in this respect. She was known to virtually everyone at the conference from her films or her various environmental and diplomatic assignments. She was popular and jauntily businesslike in her contacts and made friends easily among all delegations. In the course of some violent anti-American phrases from a Chinese speaker on the rostrum, one of his colleagues from the Chinese People's Republic was strolling past Mrs. Black's seat in the audience. Seeing her, he stopped. With a gallant bow he offered her a piece of chocolate. "What did you do?" we asked her later, when she told of the incident. "Oh, I thought it best to take it and eat it and thank him," she smiled.

Most American press representatives covered the political disturbances and generally presented the show as much ado about no real progress. We in the United States delegation, on the other hand, filed our daily cables to Washington with factual accounts of accomplishment. My State Department pals told me later that when they compared newspaper and periodical reports with our cables, they figured something was "screwy." It was. Our stay in Stockholm was an undeniable success.

After fourteen days the conference wound up with a total of 119 recommendations for national and international action, passed without objection. The world environment program had been officially born, and the blessed event was upbeat. So much so that the follow-up of the Stockholm conference has also proved fruitful, nationally and internationally.

Post-Stockholm Progress

UNITED STATES

Starting with the United States, pollution abatement programs have bounded ahead. We have powerful new control legislation on air, water (both lakes and rivers as well as clean drinking water), ocean dumping, solid waste disposal, radioactivity, pesticides, toxic substances, and noise. EPA has matured into a strong enforcement agency which monitors the quality of our air, water, and earth and enforces compliance with the standards, guidelines, and regulations it has established. Many of its decisions have already survived the test of the courts.

Although its approach has been to seek allies in the pollution war, EPA where necessary has shown its mettle on the battlefield. For example, it ordered a couple of dozen steelmakers to shut down during an emergency air pollution alert in Birmingham, Alabama; and they complied immediately. William Ruckelshaus, in the first week of the agency's existence, told three cities, Atlanta, Cleveland, and Detroit, to cease fouling their rivers, and they promptly began a schedule of pollution abatement. Pursuant to a 1972 agreement with Canada, EPA is funding billions of dollars worth of sewage treatment plants along the American shores of the Great Lakes. Already the fishing is beginning to improve in Lake Erie and Lake Michigan and the number of no-swimming days due to high coliform count in Erie is diminishing. Discouragingly, however, new contamination is appearing from toxic substances not mentioned in the pact signed by President Nixon and Prime Minister Trudeau.

All this optimism doesn't mean that the United States EPA has beaten pollution for all time. It does indicate that the vigorous and sometimes expensive measures we have taken are beginning to show results in cleaner air and water—in patches. We can anticipate greater effectiveness as the step-by-step implementation of the new laws unfolds. The cleanup machinery is in place and the public remains pretty solidly behind EPA programs.

This is not to say that there hasn't been opposition from some members of Congress and from some businesses who feel EPA standards are stricter and therefore costlier than they need be—for example, during the Arab embargo and the subsequent oil and gasoline shortage in 1974. That winter an Alaskan legislator said acidly that he wondered what EPA would say to the family of the first American to freeze to death in perfectly clean air. In the recession next year a bumper sticker read "Out of a job? Hungry? Eat an ecologist." Even an old-line federal bureaucrat growled at me the other day: "I have nothing against the environment. It's the environmentalists I don't like."

Nevertheless, EPA polls taken in 1974 and 1975 indicated that the vast majority of Americans wanted to hold onto improved environmental discipline even though it might hurt the consumer in the cost of fuel used in automobiles and power plants.

But EPA does suffer some weakness: It does not focus totally on those factors discussed in chapter 6 which may bring about massive changes in weather or climate: Pollutants from nuclear testing, fertilizers, SSTs, carbon dioxide, contrails, krypton, heat, urbanization, and desertification are of interest to EPA, but only in terms of their effects on health, not on weather and climate.

For our weather, climate, and overall environment to withstand potentially devastating change, EPA must extend its responsibility or be superseded by an agency of wider compass. Indeed, all these factors must be brought under unified, integrated, or at least harmonized controls. We need a centralized department of natural resources, or of natural resources and land use.

This department would have to coordinate its efforts with similar agencies in other governments and multinational organizations, probably the United Nations. Isn't it now axiomatic that mankind has but one biosphere, with one ocean of air, and one of salt water? We exist in one giant living room, if you will, and to disallow cigar smoking at one end of the room and permit it elsewhere is senseless, since pollutantts ultimately affect all air, weather, and climate.

We must look at what's happened outside the United States since Stockholm in order to determine how we may interlace our national controls with those of the rest of mankind. The American EPA has the best credentials for reviewing the global picture and perhaps to make tentative judgments for the future. Since it began in 1970 EPA has collaborated with every significant environmental organization in the world, both national and international.

As manager of EPA's foreign involvements for over six years I have had the good fortune to see them from a front-row seat.

Why, the reader may ask at this point, is a United States domestic regulatory agency operating outside our country? The answer is twofold: First, for reasons of efficiency we need to look at what other countries have done in environmental research and pollution control technology, and at the laws they have passed and the political and administrative know-how they have gained in handling environmental problems. We want to be sure not to reinvent the wheel—to waste resources in doing what experts elsewhere have already done. We want to get ahead as fast as we can by adopting advances made by others wherever we can find them.

To do this, we carry on a lively exchange of personal visits with many nations and organizations. We also exchange microfilm documents with more than fifty governments and multinational organizations. It is true that most of this traffic in information and people benefits the other side more than us; EPA is well ahead of most similar agencies abroad in the size and excellence of its research programs, the number and quality of its regulatory personnel, and its enforcement powers. But whatever we learn that we don't already know saves duplication here. We often send our experts on "fishing" expeditions to scout mechanical or chemical control devices or procedures in manufacturing and power plants or sewage treatment installations, when we are preparing to issue specific regulations for similar problems at home.

Second, along with the Department of State we have been following presidential policy to crusade worldwide for a cleaner, better environment. This kind of assignment, I've discovered, ignites the missionary flame in even the most phlegmatic EPA technician or scientist. He will go anywhere, anytime, to spread the word for environmental betterment. He may also be attracted by the glamor of travel to exotic places, or the wish to get away for a week or two from "the Mrs." (or "the Mr.," if the employee is a modern Ms). But like many twentieth-century Yankees, the EPA people obviously have a basic, enduring drive to share their beliefs with the unenlightened heathen overseas. It's hard to tell who's more zealous these days, our "missionaries," or those they would teach. Our experts in the United States EPA, plus those from state and city EPAs, universities, and private consulting firms, are invited to speak and write for environmental seminars in virtually every nation; also to conduct joint research. We send hundreds of EPA employees overseas annually to do these things, and turn down requests for thousands more. Many foreigners come here on their own, as if to Mecca, to sop up what EPA is doing in its numerous laboratories and in countrywide regulatory programs.

Although the Americans are leading the pack in post-Stockholm care of the environment, the movement is prospering in many countries. Indeed, a majority of both developed and developing nations have rapidly established legislative, scientific, political and administrative safeguards over the dwindling supplies of usable air, water, and soil. During an almost flash-fire reaction to the "ecology revolution," over fifty EPA-like national organizations have been established in governments. They mostly agree on these axioms:

- It is more practical to industrialize with built-in ecological safeguards at the beginning than to install retrofit machinery to clean up the mess later, as we are having to do in the United States.

- Some corrective steps are expensive, such as stack-gas scrubbers to scour the outflows from fossil-fuel-fired power plants; sewage treatment works; or devices to purify automobile exhausts. (Expense has already slowed the abatement of pollution in many poorer countries.

. The chronic fuel shortage may retard advances in environmental control, but the need to conserve energy goes hand in hand with good ecological stewardship. New energy enterprises like offshore drilling, extraction of oil from shale, or strip mining of coal can be done with minimal disruption of natural surroundings.

. Since the earth has but one reservoir of air, water, and soil, man must strive to save it in concert with his fellows—through bilateral and multilateral cooperation in research, interchange of technology, and setting mutually satisfactory standards of environmental quality. This last point is a reminder that no nation wants to have another nation's standards jammed down its throat. This doesn't rule out the possibility that one nation may voluntarily choose another's criteria. The Japanese, for example, have incorporated word for word the automobile provisions of the United States Clean Air Act amendments of 1970—provisions, by the way, which are still making some American auto makers' fur fly.

. Finally, many countries now embrace the "Polluter Pays" principle as the fairest way to fund the repair of ravaged environment. This principle has been promoted by the Organization for Economic Cooperation and Development (OECD), which includes twenty-four industrialized nations, but not the Soviet Union. It means that manufacturers foot the bill for devices to sanitize their products or manufacturing processes. It implies that the consumer, too, is a polluter if he uses the products of a factory that spews out dirty waste, or if he himself uses a product that pollutes (like a faulty automobile, power boat, or air conditioner, or a cigar). The "Polluter Pays" principle means that the added expense of pollution control is added into retail prices. Higher user charges may also be levied by municipal sewage plants that must dispose of heavy metals or other industrial toxicants in the sewage, as well as usual organic effluvia.

This summarizes the thinking of political leaders that is supported by the scientists and engineers of EPAs everywhere. The politicians inevitably keep leaving the public stage, but the technical people keep their act going for the duration of their careers; in the brief six years we have been dealing with foreign EPAs we have found this to be true in all countries. So the relationships that blossom at the professional level are the important ones (not those among the summit types) for they will form the basis for enduring cooperation. Without them, nations would be hobbled in the difficult and complex arrangements that must be made in the years ahead.

EPA's first two administrators, Ruckelshaus and Train, have encouraged these scientific and technical friendships. Both have recognized the need for planetary partnership in order to keep skies and seas clean. Both these men of exceptionable energy and charm have cut new furrows of diplomacy to start the momentum of long-term cooperation.

To comprehend how this cooperation may evolve, let's look at the environmental programs of several other countries for whom environment is a priority issue.

GREAT BRITAIN

The first environmental crisis hit Britain when the Industrial Revolution began over 150 years ago. The British concede their specific contributions to polluted air and water, but are proud of what they've done to erase them.

Two of their traditional tools have been the "alkali inspector" and the "tall stacks" plan. The "alkali inspector" was a local government official who called on managers of plants located on inland streams. Together with the manager, the inspector would decide—and still does—how much effluent the river could accept and still maintain adequate water quality.

Plagued with sulfurous fumes of factories in the Midlands, Britain erected smokestacks hundreds of feet in height. They reasoned that these tall stacks would deliver their noxious plumes high enough to ride strong prevailing breezes that would ferry them over the North Sea. There the turbulent air would dilute and disperse the unbreathable gases.

The United States EPA bases its controls on a formula something like that of the "alkali inspector"—the ability of water and air to ingest a permissible quantity of pollutant and still be of such quality that it will not injure either humans or other growing things.

However, EPA scientists don't agree with the "tall stack" policy because they can't forget that what goes up must come down, somewhere. Bad gases or particles or other poisons that threaten weather, climate, man, plants, and animals may be cleared out of one place only to cause their damage someplace else.

The Norwegians agree: Acid rain has been souring their inland lakes with the same noxious ingredients that began their journey across the North Sea on emerging from the Midlands stacks. Unverified reports blame fish kills off the southwest Norwegian coast on identical ingredients. The Swedes have also been dismayed to find pink snow falling on their fields which, when analyzed, reveals the same chemicals that rise in smoky billows from the factories of the Ruhr. Recently the British have countered with the claim that these pollutants may be coming from America.[2]

The United Kingdom's Department of the Environment (DOE) employs some 75,000 civil servants, compared to EPA's less than 10,000. The difference is due to the fact that DOE includes in its organization, large sections responsible for transportation, construction, local government, and development. The British are foresighted, for these elements must all be orchestrated some day for optimum use of land and resources. Without such integrated planning pollution control schemes must ultimately fail.

In the United States a few states have instituted land use acts, but we have yet to achieve the compromise among thousands of conflicting interests that is necessary in order to pass a national law. Of course, Britain and other European countries ran out of frontiers long before America did. As a result, they became land-use minded long before pollution became a global household word.

The United Kingdom's network of laws goes back generations and now covers most modern nuisances except auto emissions—not considered to be a major threat as yet. I don't see how any present-day visitor to London can avoid laughing (and coughing) at this assessment.

The British don't insist on such severe regulations as we do in the United States. This is because the island-dwelling British don't consider themselves as trapped as other nations by the murk of industrial urbanization. Strong ocean currents around their "tight little island" wash away pollution from the streams and brisk sea breezes carry away the emissions of tall stacks, autos, and millions of little suburban brick chimneys.

Finally, there is a connection between pollution and weather in the cleanup of London air. A complete switch from sulfurous coal to natural gas was ordered for all heating, and later there was a ban on burning wood in fireplaces. The resultant drop in the coal-dust particles meant fewer nuclei for the moisture-laden air to collect on. This is how the famous English fogs, especially the killer fogs, were stopped.

WEST GERMANY

Notwithstanding my bragging about the United States EPA, most of Europe does not perceive environmental control as a brand-new American invention. The West Germans claim they began it 400 years ago. Surely the intent was there, and with the advent of today's crushing burden of filth, some of their early laws prove remarkably up-to-date. One ancient German zoning regulation now serves to shelter residents from highway noise and auto exhausts as well as noise from neighbors.

Germany's federal program lags compared to those of the eleven "lander" (states), which carry most of the load. Our EPA is trying to shift more regulatory responsibility to the states, too, since that's where the problem starts.

Germany appears ahead of the United States in reclamation of land denuded by strip mining, and in disposal of municipal sewage and trash with an eye to recovering resources from the solids and sludge, in addition to methane gas. The methane gas caught my attention particularly on an inspection of the Berlin garbage and sludge pile. The officials took me to see a pipe they had stuck about twenty feet down into the offal. The "natural gas" that came up was strong enough to light a bright flame and to send me stumbling to my knees.

In Texas our EPA let a contract with a dairy farmer to experiment with converting cow manure into methane. A news story on this contract was headlined: "EPA BULLISH ON COW PIES."

Along with Britain, France, and Scandinavia, the Germans vigorously exchange expertise and research data with other nations. We have a formal bilateral agreement with West Germany of which I have been the United States coordinator.

FRANCE

France has created a Ministry for the Quality of Life, plus six regional river basin authorities. These authorities tax water polluters and use the taxes to finance water treatment facilities.

The first French environmental minister, Robert Poujade, was also mayor of Dijon, where the famous mustard is mixed. Sophisticated and witty, he wrote a book whose title sums up his federal environment job in mustardy tartness: *Ministry of the Impossible.*[3] The book is actually optimistic, Poujade has said, despite its title.

Central government sets policy and ninety-six prefectural departments (states) and river officials administer the laws on air, water, and oceans. Statutes have been on the books for nearly fifty years, but no air or water standards have been set. The French simply set allowable pollutant levels for particular geographic areas and leave the controls to the local authorities.

Lately the French have debated how to obtain 95 percent of their electricity needs from nuclear power by the year 2000. Legislators, scientists and administrators consulted the United States EPA on ecological susceptibilities to radioactivity.

It is clear the French care about the biosphere too. Nevertheless, like everyone else, the French do not yet know where to stash radioactive wastes from their expanding nuclear capacity. A top national utility executive said to me in semiseriousness, "We'll seal them in glass boxes, and bury them in German salt mines." Not a bad plan for a while, if the Germans agree; but ultimate disposal or reprocessing of the long-lasting material has yet to be mastered.

NORWAY

Mankind's new social disease, environmental degradation, struck Norway more like a mild allergy than an epidemic. So there was no public explosion to drive the government helter-skelter into instant remedial response—only a quiet acknowledgement that environmental degradation is an issue to focus on. Smoothly, the Norwegians forged a miltifaceted ministry in 1972 to coordinate pollution abatement, natural conservation, planning of land use, and resource management. The present minister, Mrs. Grö Harlem Brundtland, oversees most pollution programs, although the twenty-one counties (states) handle water quality enforcement. Radiation has not become troublesome, since so much power derives from hydroelectric plants, set in the country's handy network of mountains and rivers.

Per Gulden of the ministry spent a year with EPA sharing his expertise with ours. He and the lovely Mrs. Brundtland, who in private life is a housewife with three children, both told me their country's program is doing well but faces major challenges. With this word from one of the world's most unpolluted havens, we have to be cautious about accomplishments of federal programs elsewhere.

SWEDEN

Sweden's Environmental Protection Board works under the Ministry of Agriculture, with responsibilities similar to those of our EPA. Dr. Valrid Paulsen, director of the board, emphasizes that conservation dominates his forward-thinking country's efficient stewardship of its part of the biosphere. The United States EPA watches Sweden's control technology for pointers on innovations, especially in such fields as the Stockholm underground water treatment system, and the experimental toilet that flushes (allegedly!) with only a cup of liquid.

SOVIET UNION

The Soviet Union's spectacular recovery after World War II brought widespread ecological disarray. *The Spoils of Progress*, Marshall Goldman terms it in his worthwhile book by that name.[4] Dammed rivers, scores of new concrete factories, plus chemical and other industries rapidly deteriorated water and air quality in the USSR. There were no immediate countermeasures. No public protest prodded the government, as happened in America.

The Soviets have but one conservation group, and it did kick up a fuss over a paper mill's poisoning of Lake Baikal, and forced governmental controls to correct the situation. And the policy of "damn the pollution, full production ahead" began to ease in the seventies. Witness the story of Lake Sevan in Soviet Armenia.

Years ago the government earmarked this large and beautiful mountain lake for irrigating a nearby valley and furnishing hydroelectric power for much of Armenia. The engineers quickly accomplished the tremendous but necessary job of earth moving and landscape resculpting. Then in 1970 the authorities discovered that they were emptying the lake and disrupting local climate and ecosystems. Since then they've been drilling a thirty-mile tunnel to divert Arpa River water to refill the lake and restore the region.

Now, like other industrial societies, the Soviet Union has joined the parade of environmental protectionists. The USSR exerts its checkrein on pollution through several ministries, mainly in that for health, which issues environmental standards. Although the Soviets are about to establish an all-union (national) EPA, they will probably go on as they do now leaving most of the responsibility to the fifteen individual republics, all the way from legislation to the setting of standards, monitoring, and enforcement.

In 1972, before the Stockholm conference. Presidents Podgorny and Nixon signed a broad agreement on environmental collaboration between the United States and the USSR. The agreement spawned forty-one projects, spread among several United States government agencies, several of the projects inquiring into the interrelationship between pollution and weather changes. In the EPA up to 150 professionals found part-time assignments under the pact.

Academician Yuri Izrael and EPA Administrator Train comanaged the agreement. Although they tried mightily, as did the participating experts, the pact has yielded a rather random exchange of environmental data plus détente-ish friendships and ceremony, as well as lengthy, touristic trips for the leaders and their staffs. Great expectations have failed to materialize. For example, for years the USSR promised us it was about to construct two large, multimillion ruble stack-gas (SO_2) scrubbing installations for coal- and oil-burning power plants. The United States was to see all technical improvements and fresh data from this useful project— but the construction has never taken place.

In summary, the agreement was and still is a good move, even though it has yet to fulfill its potential; the habit of goodfellowship established under it will stand us in good stead for any future, more practicable arrangements.

JAPAN

Japan created its Environment Agency in mid-1971, directly under the prime minister. This executive move followed a special meeting of the Diet (Parliament) which spun a broad fabric of environmental law. Japan is now on course to cut the horrific degradation of water, air, and land caused by its postwar prosperity: industrial and vehicle pollution, overloads of sewage and urbanization. The Japanese have suffered grievous health effects from toxic substances like mercury (which caused the Minimata disease), PCBs (polychlorinated biphenyls), and cadmium (which resulted in the painful condition they called *Itai itai*—"Ouch! ouch!".

Urged by Russell Train and the Japanese minister, Sadanori Yamanaka, in 1970, United States-Japan environmental exchange and cooperation grew apace. In 1975 they flowered into a formal bilateral program approved by Foreign Minister Miyazawa and Secretary of State Kissinger.

The Japanese Environment Agency and EPA, with two of the world's toughest cleanup assignments, are continually exchanging ideas, research, and control technology. They have profited mutually in several categories: advanced waste water treatment, disposal of toxic substances, control of sulphur oxide emissions, and study of photochemical oxidants.

We EPA people marveled at how the Japanese embraced the eco-fad in 1971–72. Once the Diet and the executive branch stamped environment as "the thing," the word spread to municipal and state governments, business firms and associations, academia, and the news media. At EPA we saw this as a series of human tsunamis—visitors who frequently flooded our premises. Groups of ten to thirty would arrive and gamely endure the longest of briefings on *any* environmental topic. These cheerful, freshly minted environmentalists would then disappear in a burst of Nikon shutter clicks and courteous bows. EPA received 2,000 foreign visitors the first year of its entity and over a third were the conscientious Japanese. Their enthusiasm was reflected even at the Japanese embassy in Washington, which since 1971 has generously entertained—with oriental elegance—eco-freaks of every discipline from both countries.

CANADA

One morning at the Stockholm conference a jaunty, swashbuckling Canadian strode up and handed me a telegram. Jack Davis, his country's first environment minister, stood tight-lipped as I read the message. It told of a moderately bad (100,000 gallon) oil spill at the Cherry Point, Washington, refinery of Atlantic Rich-field Company, an American firm. The oil was flowing north at five knots in the Juan de Fuca Strait. At any moment it could be poisoning Canadian fish and landing on Canadian beaches.

Although the accident was news to me I assured the minister its consequences would be dealt with, with dispatch, under the Canadian-United States contingency plan for such emergencies. Whereupon I saw to it that a cable went to our Coast Guard to be sure they had the word and were in action. Prompt word came back that corrective measures had already begun.

Canada's EPA, "Environment Canada," is a solid organization with enforcement teeth as strong and effective as those in the United States.

Our EPA and Environment Canada have compatible programs notwithstanding the fact Canada's federal system gives greater power to the provinces than ours does to the states.

The Cherry Point incident marked only a moment in the flow of Canadian-American day-in, day-out dealings concerning our intricately intertwined ecological life as neighbors.

We can't let the steam out of every crisis as fast as we did with that spill; but along the 3,500-mile, undefended border not every problem becomes critical.

Pollution of every sort occurs, however, and our two countries are constantly and amicably sorting out each event as it arises. The biggest pollution problem of all, of course, is the alarming loss of water quality in the Great Lakes; both countries are busy, as mentioned, in a multibillion dollar thrust to restore that quality.

Canada is indeed a good neighbor, in terms set forth by the ubiquitous Maurice Strong, now president of Petro-Canada. He said that today when a nation pollutes a river that flows into another country the upstream nation is committing "environmental aggression."

From even these brief sketches of EPAs elsewhere, it should be evident that they are not equipped to overcome the full gamut of endangerments to climate, weather and, environment described in chapter 6—nor is the United States. The nations mentioned so far, along with Singapore, Hong Kong, Australia, and New Zealand, are the ones that have given priority attention to ecological difficulties.

Many countries in South America, Africa, and Asia have mounted only token, weak efforts so far. Heavily industrialized countries cook up the worst witches brew of pollution. But in the Third World, many nations have moved into a transitional period between development and nondevelopment—countries like Korea, China, India, Mexico, and Brazil. These have the worst of both ecological extremes: the lack of control typical of undeveloped states, and the excessive loading of pollutants in the air, soil, and water that characterizes the most modern municipalities and industrial centers.

INDIA

Somber thoughts depressed me on leaving India in February 1976:[5]

It's five-thirty A.M. but Bombay's airport departure lounge overflows with passengers and the sound of their coughing. These outraged lungs (plus smarting eyes and tickled noses) are reacting to that nuisance of all seasons—dirty air.

Air fouled in Bombay's outskirts by sulfurous fumes from nearby oil refineries and fertilizer plants; smoke from dry cow dung which is being burned on the sidewalks to warm the huddled poor who must sleep there; air soiled by diesel trucks and buses, coal-burning steam engines, gasoline-powered autos, and kerosene-burning airplanes—dozens of them already filling up at this airport. Planes for everywhere, as if we were fleeing some general catastrophe.

Indeed we do escape, as the Air India 707 leaps Pegasus-like into the fresh atmosphere over the Arabian Sea. Bombay's chronic pollution down below us remains. We can see it there, the smoke of a battle which is slowly killing humanity in more and more such fabulous, historic cities. How long, the dreary thought intrudes, before there is no high ground left? Already pollutant measurements show that sleepers in New York's bedroom communities of Westchester and Connecticut must breathe the downwind effluvia of the city. Was the commute worth it?

Five years ago when I was speaking for EPA in Wisconsin, a pale young woman in the audience called out fiercely, "My husband and I are *refugees* from Riverside, California. His doctor told him to leave or he would die of lung disease. When is EPA going to save Riverside?"

My observations about Bombay are antipollution, not anti-India. India is also antipollution—with a "but." At Stockholm in 1972 Prime Minister Indira Gandhi put her views before the world: She said, in effect, that we must not allow concern for environment to inhibit the march of the needy nations to industrialization.

I heard this same opinion again in Bombay, from an outstanding chemist and mother of three who doubles as air quality specialist in the National Environmental Engineering Research Institute. She agreed that Bombay must combat the tissue-scarring scourge of poisoned air. But she said, "We must make compromises in order to build the factories to furnish the jobs to feed our children." "But what's the good of your child's eating," I asked, "if he dies of emphysema?"

I cited United States figures that some 9,000 Americans expire annually from air pollutants. "Ah, but you can't really prove it was only the pollution that killed those people—and we know what starvation does. We've seen too much of its agonies here."

With that equivocal attitude India is more or less joining the ecologically committed nations.

Mahatma Gandhi made a beginning in the 1930s, but seer that he was, he warned that solutions to environment problems must be cheap enough for the people to afford them.

PEOPLE'S REPUBLIC OF CHINA

During my stay in China as a naval officer in 1946, war-weariness easily outranked pollution as a problem. Today, the People's Republic of China has, in name at least, dedicated itself to maintaining the biosphere. In 1974 it opened an environmental protection department of the State Council.

Thanks to the National Academy of Sciences program for scholarly exchanges with the People's Republic of China I was able to meet some Chinese ecologists in Washington in 1975 and 1976. What they said and what they reported on paper revealed quite a lot:

China stresses that the country must be freed from the noisome "waste gases" (as they call air pollution from industry), as well as waste water and slag. Still the government insists production plans be fulfilled—or overfulfilled.

The Chinese are using one farsighted plan to limit the poisoning of air and water: They now build only small urban complexes. This means easier control right now than in the big cities and also fewer perturbations of weather and climate, such as excessive heat, dust, CO_2, and scrambled wind patterns.

Also, the Chinese are installing antipollution equipment in plant structures, controlling excessive noise due to traffic and heavy industry, mobilizing the labor-rich population to prevent and eliminate ecological deterioration, and carrying out massive reforestation. Americans returning from China these days, including former EPA Administrator Train, speak almost in awe of the vast number of recently planted green trees.

Traditionally, human "night soil" and animal wastes are collected and used for agriculture; now methane gas is being drawn from the wastes and distributed for home heating and cooking—not an appetizing thought, but certainly this is resource recovery of the soundest sort. Yet Hong Kong is exporting to China, reportedly at considerable profit, additional large volumes of night soil. One wonders why the shortage in China; the bad taste question intrudes: Not enough to eat? This is obviously not the reason, since their government representatives concede that an unmeasured mass of untreated sewage empties into inland waterways. They are determined to remedy this sloppiness, and have already initiated a national pollution monitoring system in the large cities. But so far

THANKS, CHINA -- WE NEEDED THAT!

the Hong Kong Chinese are clearly better businessmen in this field and certainly have better-organized sewage handling.

China has been forcing its people to turn in industrial wastes for recycling: They boast of collecting one million tons in Shanghai alone in 1974. They have also clamped controls on industrial emissions of nitrogen oxide (which they call the "yellow dragon"), using as a catalyst nonnoble metals.

These commendable signs of ecological concern fade from sight whenever the Chinese open-air test another nuclear war device. Each time a hydrogen bomb blasts off in China a shower of radioactivity rides around the world's atmosphere. EPA monitors pick it up a few short days later over Nevada and elsewhere in the United States. In 1976 it contaminated milk in Pennsylvania, presumably having poisoned clouds that were about to drop rain on pastures.

How long, one wonders, before these nuclear tests damage the ozone blanket, with resulting harm to life and climate? Nevil Shute's futuristic novel *On the Beach*[6] tells the afterevents of a nuclear exchange whose radioactive miasma erases life on earth.

MEXICO

With our neighbor, Mexico, we at EPA have been trying for years in conference and in collaboration in research and training to solve common chronic pollution puzzles. Mexico's expansion of population and industry is galloping toward the kind of ghastly projections found in the Club of Rome's book *Limits to Growth*. [7]

Mexico's worst population prognostication is a jump from the present 50 million to 200 million in 1999. Urbanization and industrialization bid fair to keep pace, one indication being a constant rise in the numbers of overage, heavily smoking automobiles. Ineffective air and water pollution regulation leaves the quality of life in Mexico City, Guadalajara, and Monterrey, plus several border cities, in a steadily worsening state.

We often discussed these matters with the former Mexican environmental leaders, considering what to do and how. The results seemed to be promising. As of 1977 there's nothing much doing as yet under the new government, although its members have indicated they wish to upgrade past collaboration.

EPA has cooperated extensively with the environmental subdivision of Mexico's health ministry. In fact, in a single year, 1975, twenty-five EPA experts went to Mexico as consultants, usually through the Pan American Health Organization or the United Nations Development Program.

These contacts are healthful and useful, as both governments will agree. Nevertheless, Mexico's increasing pollution and overpopulation spell inevitable crisis. Illegal aliens are crowding into the southwest United States and the air pollution is destined to drift north increasingly. Both these factors are beginning even now to exert pressures on the United States, which can barely restrain its own excessive demand for clean air, water, living space, weather, and climate. With so far inadequate attempts to head them off, these pressures are putting the two neighbors on a collision course that will tax the talents of their scientists, leaders—and diplomats.

BRAZIL

During preparations for the Stockholm conference, Brazilians often put a stick in the spokes of the eco-movement, saying that developing countries must industrialize first and depollute later. The State Department asked me to accept an invitation to speak in the National Assembly in Brasilia in 1971. I saw close up what was really happening. The parliamentary conference started with a foreign ministry spokesman saying his set piece "It's important to worry about the environment—but later, after we've industrialized completely." Then I was allowed equal time, as an eco-freak. Gradually the meeting grew into a kind of pep rally with proenvironment talks by opinion molders from state and local governments, the law, business, science, engineering, and labor.

The conclave was terminated by an unexplained dousing of the lights, and we had to leave the chamber in darkness.

In 1976 the Brazilian government reversed field, turned on the ecological lights, and set stringent measures to preserve this greatest reservoir of natural riches left on the face of the earth. Even so, the nation will have to go further to protect the weather and climate from the rapid deforestation of the Amazonian jungle, which currently races on unchecked.

Environmental Interdependence

Today environmental isolationism is already a nonviable policy. Those who doubt this view should read a recent study of the Swedish Meteorological and Hydrological Institute which analyzed precipitation collected on Atlantic Ocean weather ships. The findings: Large amounts of man-made sulphur are being airborne from North America towards Europe. We noted earlier the travel of poisons from the United Kingdom and the Ruhr to Scandinavia. Some scientists also contend that atmospheric dirt generated in industrial Europe drifts south to the Sahel Desert, where it may have contributed to the fatal drought in the sixties that victimized people and livestock.

The conviction that all nations are enmeshed in the planet's deteriorating atmospheric and oceanic system has evoked quite a response from the major multinational organizations—NATO, for one. It was Daniel Moynihan's idea to reorient the North Atlantic Treaty Organization (NATO) to the ecological concerns of its members. This new departure for NATO began slowly. After all, to graft nonmilitary activity onto NATO would seem to invite immediate rejection; and this would have happened except that when Moynihan left the White House in 1970 Russell Train grabbed the ball. For six years, through the force of his personality and the support of several federal agencies, he demonstarted that NATO, as a functioning organization, can originate environmental initiatives. These can then be "spun off," and transferred permanently to individual members of NATO or to groups of members, if desired.

NATO's environmental projects have included comparative studies of city air pollution and of industrial effluents into a river shared by two countries, experiments in low-powered autos, conservation, earthquakes, and geothermal energy. Its program is known to participants as CCMS—the "Committee on Challenges of Modern Society."

In hard terms, critics might ask what the CCMS effort has accomplished that warrants the disproportionate effort the United States has made to drag along some not-always-so-keen member countries. At the annual plenary sessions of CCMS held in Brussels, for example, the American delegation usually numbered some two or three dozen persons compared to the average of three or four sent from the other capitals—and they didn't have to cross an ocean to get there. All kinds of additional meetings and trips were conjured up to give impetus to the program. At today's transportation prices, plus expenses for each traveler, not to mention time away from their regular government jobs, the cost to the American taxpayers for the CCMS campaign and the Soviet agreement combined has been several millions of dollars. Yet one cannot pinpoint any specific long-term technical achievements from either of these heavily staffed exercises. Both were hand-created and operated by Russell Train, who is deservedly popular and powerful among United States environmental circles, including the loyal supporters among the press.

On balance I believe these big programs led personally by Train, as well as many others handled routinely by EPA and the State Department, are worth the taxpayers investment. The real goal is a promotional one. These activities have resulted in considerable publicity each step of the way. They directly involve thousands of foreigners. In the environmental movement, which is vital to the survival of all of us, ballyhoo and advertising are needed to spread our own dedication abroad. When American and overseas environmental experts share their know-how on the spot, the effect can be immediate.

Robert Poujade, the French environment minister, dubbed EPA chief Train an "apostle of the environment." This is accurate, and it applies to the hundreds of EPA and other agency personnel who have accompanied Train or followed his lead to so many corners of the world.

In the early seventies the specialized agencies of the United Nations hurried to expand their "empires" into the newly recognized territory of environment. The World Health Organization and the World Meteorological Organization each created its own environmental program.

After the Stockholm meeting of 1972 the United Nations Environment Program (UNEP) was formed and the 1972 United Nations General Assembly voted a five-year budget of $100 million. Maurice Strong was the unanimous choice to be executive secretary. In order to secure the support of emerging nations for the enterprise, the headquarters were located in Nairobi, Kenya.

At the end of the first four years, the program moved to catalyze environmental research, information exchange, and other cooperative steps toward clearing up the global environmental mess.

The tidiest example of multilateral counterattack on pollution is a pact among the four Scandinavian nations. It simply extends the liability of a polluter in any of the four countries to each of the other three. If a power plant in one country allows poisonous fumes from its stack to drift into a town across the border, that town can sue the plant in the country where it is located just as if they were both under the same flag.

Can we expect planetary management of human and natural pollution any time soon? I think the answer is yes. Cooperative activity has been going on at ever increasing speed in this decade. It presages international control machinery that before long may be as good as that of the International Postal Union or the International Telecommunications Union. But first, national EPAs must expand their domains. At present their purview only extends to local air, water, and soil—and humans, plants, and animals. Ultimately the environmental arms of government must control activities that affect our weather, our climate, and the global ocean.*

* Under the Ocean Dumping Convention of 1973 and the 1954 convention on the prevention of pollution of the sea by oil, some international law is in force to preserve the global ocean; but nations are only just beginning to set up implementative machinery.

8

DIPLOMATIC AND LEGAL BYPLAY

In Harm's Way?

Increasing our mastery of weather, climate, and environment doesn't please everyone, I have learned. In fact, it has begun to cause trouble because of feared effects on bystanders, innocent or not, at home or abroad.

When trouble looms in our society, lawyers get busy. The pursuit of weather modification in the United States has already given rise to a spate of laws and lawsuits. These have added cash to the coffers of environmental law firms, but mostly confusion for those who may be subject to harm from experimental or commercial cloud seeding. What about the well-intentioned weather modifier who wants to avoid harassing lawsuits by those who mistrust his operations? The latest legal lore doesn't give him much guidance either.

When the environment is soiled, roiled, or despoiled across borders these days foreign offices put their diplomats to work on the matter. Indeed they start work before any real damage occurs, signing agreements or at least negotiating. They feel foresight is essential to defend against the unpredictable potential of tinkering with weather and climate, and especially of environmental warfare.

Legal Status of Weather Modification in the United States

Let's look first at the legal status of weather manipulation in our own country. It's a short story, but significant: By 1974 NOAA announced that twenty-eight states had already instituted regulations to control weather modification. A majority of these states won't allow an individual or firm to conduct "weather mod" operations without written permits, secured by means of full disclosure of their plans, and payment of a fee. The licenses issued to weather modifiers range in cost from $10 in North Dakota to $200 in Nebraska. These amounts are, of course, subject to revision upwards as inflation mounts and state revenues diminish in real value. The individual states which have such requirements are principally those where drought, hail, and fog tend to drain the economy, and where farmers and businessmen seeking relief from them might be bilked by unscrupulous operators in the absence of governmental attention. Vincent Schaefer in 1962 excoriated those who "preyed on the relative ignorance and desperate situation of groups of farmers and ranchers, mulcting them of hundreds of thousands of dollars."[1]

Taking out insurance is one course open to those who may be menaced by weather modification: Who knows whether he is apt to be drowned or blown down or whatever by weather work gone awry? However, since rainmakers themselves still can't give statistical evidence of their positive accomplishments, it is hard to estimate the possibilities of their spreading havoc somewhere downwind of their operations.

I have inquired among insurers how they handle this matter in their industry. So far their replies have been vague. One probable reason for their diffidence is the catastrophic storm that struck Rapid City, South Dakota, in early June 1972. Although the Stockholm Conference on the Human Environment was then under way, we conferees heard not a word about how one group of weather modifiers allegedly laid waste the human environment in the Black Hills. But lawyers, insurance men, and injured clients have been talking about the event ever since.

In the afternoon of June 9, Project Skywater, conducted by the South Dakota School of Mines of the United States Department of Interior's Bureau of Reclamation, dispatched some cloud-seeding planes. They flew through the clouds over Sturgis, just north of Rapid City, and scattered over 500 pounds of nucleating salt. The rains came beyond all expectations—and came and came. A giant storm followed. It wound up as one of this country's worst calamities. The question that still rages is, who caused it—God or man? The combination of cloud burst and flash flood was complicated by the breaking of Canyon Lake Dam. The toll was hideous: 238 persons dead, and hundreds of millions of dollars worth of property damage. The aftereffects of Rapid City lasted for over three years, and involved $63 million in government emergency grants. Quite an ordeal for a city of 47,000 people.

The Rapid City case still ranks as the biggest example of costly damage allegedly resulting from rainmaking or other types of atmospheric alteration. As the technology of rainmaking improves, safeguards must be found to prevent such ricochet effects. Only then will rainmaking become as acceptable a way to obtain fresh water as digging wells or tapping lakes, rivers, and reservoirs.

Meanwhile, there are other difficulties. For example, what can be done to allay the concern of some people that it is tempting the wrath of the Deity to mess around with the basic forces of weather and climate? Or more scientifically speaking, should we dare to try to change the weather when we don't understand it well enough even to forecast it? So far these concerns have not led to any laws

that obstruct weather modification, although a related one probably will—that is, a widespread worry that enhancing precipitation
in one community can be done only at the expense of the normal
precipitation in another. Unless it can be proved that rainmaking is
not robbing Peter to pay Paul, there will doubtless be more cases
like that of the Maryland farmer who spotted a commercial cloud
seeder circling over a neighbor's property. He was sure that the
seeding would intercept rain he wanted for his fields. So he revved
up his jeep, sped as close to the plane as he could, and fired
shotgun pellets at the pilot until he flew away.

There will always be the dilemma of one man's meat being the
other's poison. When New York State suffered a severe drought in
the middle fifties a commercial cloud seeder was hired to end it.
Everyone agreed this was sensible—except one resort owner, who
pointed out that wet weather would drive away vacationers. He
was more genteel than the Marylander. He merely threatened a
lawsuit to reclaim the tourist revenues he would lose if the clouds
should give birth to rain following their artificial insemination with
silver iodide.

If rainmakers bring rain or wind in areas outside their intended
targets then the most likely recourse for those damaged will be the
"class action" suit, now so popular in fighting against pollution.

Ways of handling such problems are now becoming more regu-
larized. Weather modification activities are increasingly herded
toward the corral of federal control. By law, NOAA already
requires all weather modification operators, whether governmental or private, to report annually what they have done (or tried
to do) during the year. NOAA's Environmental Modification Office in Rockville, Maryland, publishes this information annually.
The 1975 report listed projects conducted in seventy-four different
locations in the United States. Despite the scientific and popular
controversy over their practicability, these "weather mod" activities are widespread.

NOAA is gently nudging the operators into a sense of responsibility. They must file an environmental impact statement before

any project commences. They must also describe the safety measures to be taken, even though such measures generally presuppose more knowledge of the technology than exists. Nevertheless, NOAA's insistence that "weather mod" performers look before they leap should go far to avoid the legal tangles that plague the fledgling profession at its present stage.

Diplomacy and Environmental Modification

So far NOAA has no international counterpart to keep environmental modification honest and safe, though the idea of one came up informally at the Stockholm conference. I did hear rumors there of far-out experiments and large-scale projects being contemplated. Officially, Principle 21 of the Final Declaration of the conference hints at international discipline over "en mod," though it is not mentioned by name: "Nations have . . . the responsibility to ensure that activities within their jurisdiction or control do not cause damage to the environment of other states or of areas beyond the limits of national jurisdiction." The framers of this language doubtless had transboundary pollution mostly in mind, but it applies to environmental modification, too. So does international law, according to a couple of legal consultants who advised the State Department in 1968: Citing the Corfu Channel Case of 1949, Rita and Howard Taubenfeld said flatly that international law requires a country "not to allow knowingly its territory to be used for acts contrary to the rights of other states."

The day when good fences make good neighbors has gone forever, in terms of environmental modification—unless someone can erect a fence of an impenetrable substance like glass, sink it into the ground beneath the rivers and water tables, and raise its top above the stratosphere.

Bilateral precautions have begun against possible negligence on the part of modifiers of weather, climate, and other aspects of the environment. Canada and the United States started the vogue with the world's first weather modification agreement in 1974. It is rather loose, calling mainly for talks between the countries before either one commences weather modification activities that could spread into the other. This means any action within 200 miles of the international boundary. It also applies to "weather mod" anywhere in either country if, in the judgment of either side, it may "significantly affect the composition, behavior or dynamics of the atmosphere" across the border.

This friendly understanding suffered some strain when the United States government learned by accident that Canada was determined to drill the Beaufort Sea bed next to Alaska in the summer of 1976. Canada hadn't mentioned the plan to the United States when, embarrassingly, it surfaced in the press as the Canadian Parliament prepared to render the final decision on whether to go ahead, whereupon the diplomats and representatives of the two environmental agencies met and reviewed the estimates of potential harm that an oil well break, particularly one under the ice, would bring about. Canadian scientists had delved carefully into the possibilities of disrupting the region's plant and animal life. In fact, they completed more than forty separate environmental impact studies.

We of the United States communicated our nation's official concern and the Canadians promised to maintain the strictist precautions. Sometimes the Beaufort Sea doesn't thaw for two or three years in a row. If a blowout occurred just before freezing, there could be quite a black hemorrhage under the ice before the next thaw. Finally the Canadian Parliament gave the green light and drilling took place, fortunately without incident. The ease and speed with which the two countries defused this explosive issue bodes well for the future handling of weather modification difficulties that may arise between neighbors as the new technology grows in scope.

Senator Claiborne Pell of Rhode Island proposed a far-reaching plan for the international control of weather modification. He didn't want to just leave control simply to a veiled mention by the Stockholm conference or to limited agreements between only two at a time of the world's 154 nations to be careful about the downwind or downstream dangers of "en mod." In 1976 Senator Pell asked for a specific international treaty under which a nation planning "en mod" projects that could affect land, sea, or air outside its own sovereignty would prepare an environmental impact statement for international scrutiny.

The proposing of treaties is constitutionally a responsibility of the executive branch, with the Senate "advising and consenting"; but nothing *forbids* Senate initiative. In 1966 Senator Pell had already become the first United States senator to compete with the State Department as a treaty writing font. Here's how it happened:

Senator Pell's bill to establish Sea Grant colleges for the promotion of knowledge of marine resources had just been signed into law by President Johnson. Casting about for other sea-related tasks, Senator Pell (who was once a Foreign Service officer) thought of two recent, precedent-breaking treaties: One ensured the peaceful exploration of outer space and the other, nonbelligerent development of the Antarctic. The senator wondered, What about "ocean space"?

Beyond the territorial sea boundaries there is a vast, relatively unexplored, and commercially unexploited region of ocean bottom. This subsea area encompasses nearly three quarters of the earth's surface. Untold mineral riches sit ready for the taking, on or beneath the ocean floor.

Beyond the coastal sections of seabed that are claimed and policed by adjacent mainland powers there lay a great security vacuum. Shouldn't there be a covenant to discourage further military exploitation of the open area? We could call it a "treaty for the peaceful uses of ocean space," mused the senator.

The first step in his strategy was to consult with the departments of State and Defense to seek their "advice and consent." At first, each department was horrified.

At the beginning it looked as if the senator would be thrown out at first base. I know: I was his agent in the conversations with State and Defense. But it was politic to have the support of these departments for the Senate resolution through which Pell would announce his idea; and Senator Pell has a stoic patience that is in keeping with his partial American Indian heritage.

Within a year (1967) the Senate resolved in favor of his draft treaty, with the sufferance and then the active support of the State Department. I remember the first call I made at State: It was a meeting with the department's scientific advisor, Herman Pollack. As I delivered my message, I sensed that I was close to being ushered out of his office. But within months Mr. Pollack delivered a speech touting the treaty. Out of our interchange a warm friendship grew up between us.

The Defense Department also dropped its objections. The Johnson administration soon brought the treaty proposal to the attention of the United Nations General Assembly. In 1968 Pell's single-mindedness achieved worldwide approval—a United Nation agreement to disallow weapons of mass destruction on the international seabed.

Early in 1972 Senator Pell once again asked his colleagues to usurp what had always been the responsibility of the president and the secretary of state. This time he proposed a Senate resolution for a treaty to ban environmental or geophysical modification as a weapon of war. The senator added that the military use of weather modification would jeopardize the United States' hard-won cooperation with the scientists of other nations in vital, long-range weather forecasting. Many scientists both in and out of government concur with the senator on this point.

It is imperative, he concluded, that the United States dedicate all environmental and geophysical modifications programs to peaceful purposes. If we don't prohibit military application of this growing technology the "way has been left open to the planning, development, and prosecution of deliberate environmental or geophysical warfare."

Pell attracted support from a broad spectrum of leaders and experts.

Today I believe the most credible witnesses for a ban on environmental war are the scientists. They understand the research, the experiments, and the theory involved. To a man (and a woman—Dr. Joanne Simpson), they warn against environmental war with all their considerable knowledge and prestige. "We're against it," say the eminent thinkers in science—meteorologists, mathematicians, ecologists and others, people like Reid Bryson of the University of Wisconsin, Stephen Schneider of the National Center for Atmospheric Research, Joseph Smagorinsky, chief of NOAA's Geophysical Fluid Dynamics Laboratory, Edith Brown Weiss and Richard Falk of Princeton, and Dr. Gordon F. MacDonald of Dartmouth.

To date, Dr. Edward Teller may be the only scientist who is a naysayer on the subject of a treaty. He has told me that although he is against using environmental modification for military advantage he favors an information exchange rather than a diplomatic pact against development of weather or other environmental weaponry.

In September 1974 the Soviets unexpectedly presented a double package at the United Nations General Assembly: a resolution and draft treaty designed to stop environmental war at its current embryonic stage. In mute salute to Senator Pell, the Soviet wording closely resembled his. But the timing caught our State Department off guard. Although Pell's Senate resolution had passed in July of 1973, State had not instituted any diplomatic follow-up.

In fact, probably because of the Defense Department's foot-dragging, the Pell-proffered treaty was going nowhere. Nevertheless, companion resolutions in the House of Representatives under Gilbert Gude and Donald Fraser helped keep the treaty idea alive with more hearings.

Now, ironically, the Soviets had produced the prod for State and Defense to get their ducks in a row for a unified administration position. This accomplished, in November 1974 the Soviets and Americans held the first of three bilateral talks. Then the following August they submitted identical texts to the Conference of the Committee on Disarmament (CCD) in Geneva.

The CCD consists of thirty nations that have been patiently striving for disarmament since 1961. Their progress has been remarkable. In that time they've scored four solid achievements: the Nuclear Nonproliferation Treaty, the Biological Warfare Convention, the (Pell) Seabed Treaty, and the Limited Test Ban. As co-chairmen of the CCD, the Americans and Soviets possessed the leverage for persuading others to join a ban on environmental war.

If one listened to the declamations against environmental war by Ambassador Jacob Malik when he enunciated the Soviet resolution at the United Nations, one would have put the Soviets on the side of Pell, Argentina, and Mexico, in favor of the most stringent control. Excerpts from his remarks show him overzealous on the present state of peaceful weather modification applications: "Scientists of a number of countries have succeeded in considerably reducing wind velocity and the destructiveness of hurricanes. . . . In fact, boundless possibilities for mankind are being opened up by the peaceful, creative use of scientific discoveries to influence the environment and climate in the interests of mankind and in order to improve its well-being."

Malik also overstated the present power and scope of environmental weaponry. He spoke, with a certainty which the facts don't quite bear out, of the impact of cloud seeding in Vietnam, such as "excessive precipitation resulting in the inundation of terrain, in landslides, in the destruction of roads, dikes, bridges, and so on."

He also mentioned that man can create extensive ultraacoustic and infraacoustic fields. "Infrasound," as he called it (with its frequencies lying below human audibility) can "cause complete mental derangement," and can also be employed to create acoustic fields on the sea and the ocean surface to combat individual ships or whole flotillas. Finally, he drew attention to man-made tidal waves capable of "wiping off the face of the earth many coastal cities and whole areas."

In December 1976 the CCD text came up for a vote and won overwhelming Assembly approval as a "convention" or treaty. The United Nations convention now aligns the world against environmental warfare. Another victory for Senator Pell's facsimile State Department on Capitol Hill.

It may be a great victory for mankind, too.

Back in August 1976, Senator Pell had written Senate Resolution 521 for his third draft treaty—this time requiring statements of international environmental impact. Pell's next treaty would disallow any activity that might significantly affect the environment of other nations or a global commons area until reviewed by the office of the United Nations Environment Program.

Pell specified six categories of activities to illustrate why he thinks a treaty is called for: transportation, energy production, resource development (including sources of energy), waste disposal, disaster prevention, and food production. Pell pointed out that each of these generates detrimental ecological impacts locally and internationally. For examples he cited ocean dumping of radioactive wastes from the mushrooming number of nuclear power plants; oil pollution from the world's merchant marine, which has grown from 14,600 vessels with a tonnage of 121,900,000 in 1954 (when the Convention for the Prevention of Pollution of the Sea by Oil was passed) to 22,900 vessels of 556,600,000 tons in 1975; and the unpredictable spin-offs from trying to prevent natural disasters like hurricanes and earthquakes. Pell warned that "storm steering, the release of geological tensions, and modulation of precipitation may be possible in the future, but the confinement of the results of such activities to one nation may be impossible."

At this writing Pell's 1976 treaty offering appears to be somewhat mired. But my guess is that with the environmental war pact implemented he will recommence slugging away at the governmental inertia which is slowing the new pact.

9

FAIR WEATHER AHEAD

Living beside the sea, as I do, tends to turn you into a sort of human barometer, meteorological litmus paper, or one-man almanac; the problem is to get anyone to listen to you. You note the winds, cloud shapes, temperature, state of the sea, and humidity. As a naval officer I was trained to do all this while on watch aboard ship and enter my observations in the log. After a while you hardly need to glance at anemometers, thermometers, and other devices: The Lord has given us flesh sensors that pick up all this information. When I do check the instruments I generally find no surprises. With this mix of physiological and Abercrombie and Fitch equipment an interested beach dweller can nearly always tell what weather's coming, without checking the press reports.

In previous chapters we have talked about indicators of the world's weather, climate, and environment with special focus on what man can do to affect them. Insofar as we can, we like to determine our own future; and the way we run our lives today is going to figure into any prediction on the future state of our surroundings. As mentioned, we already have levers by which, intentionally or unintentionally, we alter certain aspects of the air, sea, and land, both positively and negatively.

At the outset I promised to make no predictions, but only to give enough information to the reader to make his own forecast of what lies ahead. To assist him in that process I will conclude by identifying the fields which can provide the best telescope for looking at our tomorrows. We can observe the sayings of scientists, energy use, food production, environmental modification by large-scale projects to move earth or sea or ice, weather modification, environmental warfare, pollution control, climate, and future growth.

Sayings of Scientists

In the past twenty years sages of many scientific disciplines—such as economics, meteorology, climatology, biology—have been bombarding us with dire predictions as to our fate in the near future. One book, *Famine, 1975!,*[1] assured us that projected curves of population growth and food growth would be passing each other in 1975, each in the wrong direction. This meant with millions of people starving a probable resort to "triage" would be called for. (Triage was a way of sorting wounded in World War I: They were divided into three categories—those who could survive without treatment, those who would die even with treatment, and those who could be saved if treated.) In distributing her agricultural surpluses, the authors said, America would have to practice a form of triage, since there would not be enough for everyone. The book was right to the extent that people have been dying of starvation by the hundreds of thousands in Asia and Africa. For example, in 1972 India's decrease in food production, combined with population pressures, "probably claimed well over a million lives."[2] The full catastrophe has not arrived on schedule, thank heaven; but this of course doesn't rule it out for later on.

The Club of Rome's report of 1972[3] also set up a scarecrow to frighten people into recognizing the "limits to growth" and the painful ecological consequences of *not* slowing down growth. In this report the days of predicted doom still await us, falling at the turn of the century or later. But scientists at EPA found this report to be based on "soft" data in many instances and hence not a totally reliable piece of work.

The inaccuracies of these two publications can be excused if you agree that the trends they describe are so menacing they should be exaggerated in order to persuade people to stop them in time.

In the mid-seventies a plethora of books, magazines, and press pieces have been bombarding us ordinary citizens with worries about anthropogenic overheating of the atmosphere at one end of the spectrum of horrors, and a hurry-up return to a new Ice Age at the other. Definite climate changes have been forecast based on all kinds of possible causes: the elliptical shape of the earth's orbit about the sun; the wobble of the earth's axis (like that of a spinning top slowing down); sun spots; and whatnots.

I won't try to winnow out the good from the bad in this recent rash of revelations. Since several of them contradict each other, however, it is clear that they are not all correct. We can accept the fact that some may be wrong; after all, these scientists are tussling with topics that have ranked as imponderables for generations. What is too bad (and what should disqualify some scientists from serious attention by government decision makers) is that a careless few seem to be headline hunters rather than guardians of the scientist's flame of truth.

Certain contemporary scientists, being aware of public interest in a given issue, hurry to publish "the answer" in order to be the first on the scene—when all they've got to show is two or three points on a graph. From these they project a curve of confident prophecy, although their data are clearly insufficient to back up their pronouncements.

Adlai Stevenson, for whom I was once spokesman at the United Nations, liked to say that "flattery is harmless, if you don't inhale." Well, the same thought applies to some scientists and to publicity.

I asked Professor Joseph Smagorinsky of Princeton about the proclivity of some of his colleagues to "go public" too fast. He says the way to avoid misleading the man in the street is not to quash the advocate of some half-baked new principle, but to urge him to present his theories first to his professional peers. They know what questions to pose to elicit the essential answers—something the curious layman is not equipped to do. Samgorinsky insists he is not calling for a complete scientific consensus. This is meaningless, he declares. "Truth is truth, and how many scientists or anyone else agrees with it is not really relevant."

Reid Bryson, geophysicist and sometime rhymist, concurs: "I will not bow to consensus science / The truth's too often in defiance."

For the political managers of our society, consensus is important, though not overridingly so, in making sound decisions. The scientist who counsels these managers needs to be thorough and to weigh all the evidence objectively. Otherwise he will leave the leaders who depend on him standing on the quicksand of conjecture rather than the bedrock of fact.

In these perilous years it would be fitting, I think, to devise a sort of Hippocratic Oath for the scientists on whose word our future may rest. This might cut down the column inches of self-advertising which a few irresponsibles have been able to get by giving a tiny portion of the truth, not the whole truth.

The majority of scientists of course don't fit this shoe. But those who do sour the credibility of the solid ones. Unfortunately some of those who are most print-prone are also the brightest. If they'd stick to their chosen profession and eschew that of publicist, the citizenry might learn the full answers more quickly. Meanwhile we need to pick carefully, these days, in the vineyard of scientific theory.

Meteorology being one of the key sciences relevant to this book, I talked to many of its practitioners about their field, its ethos, and its peculiarities. What a small group of meteorologists there is! Reid Bryson recalled that before World War II only a couple of dozen existed in this country. Bryson himself held only the thirtieth Ph.D. in the subject.

Then World War II produced large numbers of meteorologists to foretell weather for military operations. That's how Irving Krick made his name. He told General Eisenhower that June 6, 1944, would be a fair enough day for invading Normandy. Later he was retained by Ike's aide C. Langhorne Washburn to advise him on weather for the huge political rallies being planned to get the general elected president. Washburn said that Krick never missed once, in at least a half dozen events.

Yet one of my war-trained meteorologist friends informed me that after World War II it was mainly those students who couldn't make it in the "hard" sciences who picked meteorology. Some doubters say that nowadays young men (and women) go into the clergy for similar reasons—they can't make it in the tough, competitive walks of life.

I asked my meteorologist informant how he could say such things against the reputation of his lifelong occupation. For argument's sake I threw in the thought that—just as with clergymen, on whom millions of faithful count for spiritual guidance—scores of millions look to the daily estimates of the weatherman before going out to work or play. Furthermore, farmers and ranchers must glean from meteorologists' counsel whether we face a new Ice Age, or a decade of drought. Finally, there are a feisty few among meteorologists who have the intellectual courage to challenge present shaky scientific opinion on weather and climate modification. They may well be the meteorological Moses to lead us to the "promised climate" where man himself can command either rain or sunshine, to suit his needs.

My friend the meteorologist seemed unabashed by my verbal gusher. "OK," said he, "there were some good meteorologists even during this sparse period. Anyhow, there's a fine new crop, now that the profession has become so prominent in the public mind."

Better Energy Use

Dr. William S. von Arx is a typical respected scientist who publishes his views and findings only after going over his figures with the precision of a Swiss watchmaker.* For example, it took him three years—from 1973 to 1976—to collect and verify the numbers on one sheet of paper. It is a rather special page (Table 2), listing as it does the total power naturally available for use on this earth.

Incidentally, it is only normal for a nontechnical man at EPA (as I was) to comment on the slowness with which some scientists advance their views; at EPA the administrative types often beat on the necks of scientists like jockeys on racehorses to speed up their research backup data for the pollution control standards and regulations, which have to be issued on schedule.

As a sixtyish senior scientist at the Woods Hole Oceanographic Institute, Dr. von Arx does not need any riding crop on his neck; he is an urgent man who believes that the supply of natural power is adequate to any reasonable demand by man and that we should be busy figuring out how to lay our hands on it.

In looking at Table 2, the reader should know that the mathematical shorthand term "10^2," meaning "ten times ten" or "ten to the second power" stands for 100; and from there on each increase of one in the exponent means another zero added at the end of the written-out number ("10^3" means 1,000, and so on). The amount von Arx gives for direct solar power hitting the earth's surface is 10^{16} watts, or 10,000,000,000,000,000 watts—ten quadrillion watts! A much higher amount of direct solar power reaches the top of the atmosphere: 10^{17} watts. This is in the order of ten times greater than that received at the surface, because our cloud cover both absorbs and reflects away a large percentage of the incoming rays before they reach the earth's surface. The figures here are broad estimates of the relative orders of magnitude of power in the

---

* In fact he *is* Swiss, with citizenship both in Switzerland and in the United States.

Table 2: ESTIMATES OF POWER LEVELS IN NATURAL PROCESSES
OF THE PLANET EARTH*

	Total Power in Watts
1. *Available Sources of Power*	
Direct solar power	
Where sun hits atmosphere	10^{17}
At earth's surface	10^{16}
Photosynthesis (Stores sunlight, in the form of chemical energy, in fats, proteins, and carbohydrates—all combustible.)	
Marine plants	10^{14}
Arable lands, forests	10^{13}
Bioconversion of waste materials	
Plant residues and manure (Can be converted by bacteria to gaseous fuels—hydrogen and methane —by storing them in airless containers at proper temperatures.)	10^{12}
Garbage, sewage, and pulps (Can be converted by the same process.)	10^{12}
Ocean thermal power	
Solar heat absorbed by ocean water (Can possibly be put to use by exploiting temperature differences between surface and depths, producing power to drive turbines.)	10^{13}
Steady surface-wind power, like that from trade winds (Atolls would provide one good place to put windmills.)	10^{12}
Variable surface-wind power (in middle latitudes where winds are unsteady)	10^{12}
Hydroelectric power (from harnessing the kinetic energy of moving waters)	
Power in rainfall (Conceivably could be harnessed; but the world's total rainfall—even if you include the rain dropping on the oceans—would satisfy only 10 percent of the world's power demand.)	10^{12}
Flow of rivers (Harnessable by traditional hydroelectric plants)	10^{11}

	Total Power in Watts

1. *Available Sources of Power*

Natural evaporative exchanges between large bodies of water (Mediterranean Sea and Red Sea are examples: evaporation is greater in them than in the ocean at large; therefore, there is a continual flow into them from the oceans to replace evaporated water. This flow can be harnessed, just as in a mill race.) 10^9

Damming of evaporative sinks. (By damming ocean openings to Red Sea and Mediterranean Sea, letting these seas evaporate until a drop of 100 meters or more occurs, and then letting the ocean flow in, turning mill wheels, additional power might be obtained. Not very practicable to build these dams, however.) 10^{11}

Tidal flow (Particularly at places like the Bay of Fundy, where flow can be harnessed.) 10^9

Power of great ocean currents like the Gulf Stream and Kuroshio Current. (Theoretically these can be harnessed the way rivers are, with some sort of "water wheel.") 10^8

Ocean surface waves at coastline (Power of waves is available at a potential total yield of 10^6 watts per kilometer of coastline.) 10^{10}

Geothermal power (Particularly at the "ring of fire" around the Pacific Ocean basin, so called because this is where tectonic plates merge and volcanoes erupt; the same happens along mid-ocean ridges.) 10^{10}

2. *Present Power Demands*

Worldwide power demand for all needs of civilization 10^{13}

Human metabolism (Total power in terms of food needed to sustain present population level of 4 billion.) 10^{11}

* Some of the information of this table has appeared in the July 1974 issue of *Oceanus*, a publication sent to associates of the Woods Hole Oceanographic Institution and *EOS*, Vol. 55, No. 9, September 1974.

various processes of nature. They are going on anyway, and all we have to do is be smart enough to use them.

Table 2 has been adapted from William S. von Arx's estimates made during the years 1973–76. Dr. von Arx has tried to show as briefly as possible some important sources of energy other than fossil fuels and nuclear plants—sources which are renewable and which are available to solve the present and long-term energy crunch.

Let's look at power in the simplest terms:

Running an auto uses	100,000 watts
Keeping a house warm takes	10,000 watts
Reading a book requires	
Light bulb:	100 watts
Keeping body warm:	100 watts
Total:	200 watts

Therefore to save energy we need merely to stay home, put on thermally insulated clothes, and read a book.

Von Arx points out in an article[4] packed tight with solutions to the energy shortage that meeting the total world's present power demand, 10^{13} watts (it must be understood that most of the energy we produce comes from combustion of fossil fuels), is adding only 0.1 percent to the solar energy reaching the earth's surface. This is too small an increment to affect the climate or weather, except possibly in the heat islands centered around large cities. However, warns von Arx, if we up our energy use to 10^{14} or 10^{15} watts, this will add respectively 1.0 percent to 10.0 percent to the total heat already being received from the sun. At that level of additional heat input by man, "significant alterations of climate could ensue." Neither von Arx, nor Howard Wilcox (who expatiates on the terrible consequences of overheating this planet in *Hothouse Earth*)[5] nor anyone else can spell out exactly how beneficial or detrimental these changes would be. But von Arx says we can avoid them if we will simply develop these sources mentioned in his table that don't produce new heat in the atmosphere.

Von Arx lives his own life in harmony with this idea. He has built a snug little wooden house perched on a hill overlooking the town of Woods Hole, Massachusetts. He has accoutered it with simple chemical and mechanical means for converting natural energy into useful forms and returning it to the environment as heat—which it would have become anyhow in the normal course of events. The day I visited him a modernistic windmill whirred silently in the twenty-five-knot Cape Cod breeze; black solar panels picked up the September sunlight inside his little greenhouse, to keep his vegetables' roots warm at night and heat the water for his bath. Inside the house were books and papers on countless additional schemes he follows personally to expedite civilization's liberation from dependence on fossil fuels.

Von Arx has been talking of an energy-saving sequence which encompasses Aristotle's notion of a unified world comprising earth, air, fire, and water in permanent harmony. Using a windmill (*air*) he would pump *water* from a well, heat it by the sun (*fire*), and return it to the well, which is of course encased in soil (*earth*). He believes the earth will insulate the water and keep it warm. The point of the sequence would be to see whether water once warmed by solar rays can be kept at a high temperature and used again for heating a house or bathwater, or for other domestic or commercial purposes.

Actually such an experiment was done in a sewage treatment plant at nearby Otis Field (the USAF air base). After six months, water which had been solar-heated to 70°F and then allowed to percolate down to a well was pumped to the surface once more. A thermometer was promptly stuck into it, then lifted, and it read 70°F!

Von Arx and his associates are ecstatic at the efficacy of this method for heating and storing water, which is costless (except for the cost of the original equipment) and which they feel can capture and store energy for a multitude of potential uses.

Von Arx concedes that not all the sources he lists in his table offer immediate practicable alternatives. For example, the collection and conversion of solar energy, though attractive because it is clean, abundant, and replenishable, are still too expensive and complex for countrywide adoption. The Carter administration has already recognized the limits of the technology and the high cost of this substitute for oil, gas, and coal.

The Mitre Corporation has concluded that solar energy could satisfy the needs of 20 billion or more persons, each using energy at a higher rate than at present; and could do it without any impact on the climate from the release of waste heat, carbon dioxide, and particulates.[6] Mitre agrees with von Arx that climate changes might result from the absorption of solar energy on the huge collectors that would be needed, wherever it may be used.

But until such negative results can be predicted with certainty, such opponents of nuclear and fossil fuel as von Arx, Amory Lovins, friends of the Earth, Henry Kendall of MIT, and William E. Heronemus of the University of Massachusetts will continue to fight for the use of energy that is renewable. To consume in one century, as we are doing, what took hundreds of millions of years to evolve is an "outrage," von Arx told me fiercely. We have a perfect substitute, he went on; and Clarence Zener has been a leading thinker in showing its value:

Our biggest repository of solar energy is stored as heat in the subtropical oceans. If released, in one second these could yield 10^{28} watts, says von Arx. In order to get at this unbelievably rich trove of energy, the United States Energy Research and Development Administration (ERDA) is now subsidizing the development of a system called OTEC. OTEC means "Ocean Thermal Energy Conversion." It operates like a Rankine cycle engine, meaning that it employs a closed loop of pipes in which a gas is circulated. In the OTEC version pipes are filled with a refrigerant, either propane or ammonia, which will change from liquid form to gaseous form if there is at least 25°F rise in temperature, then back again when the temperature falls that much. So in the OTEC cycle the liquefied refrigerant is pumped up from the deep cold water to the warm water at the surface, where it boils into vapor which (like steam) then drives a turbine. When the gas is shoved down through the pipe again to the cold deep water it condenses once more into a liquid. Whereupon the cycle is repeated. The amount of power taken off by the turbine is vastly greater than the minimal quantity necessary to pump the gas around the enclosed system of pipes.

The tropical waters are the ideal location for OTEC. In the first place, as Professor Heronemus explains, they constitute a huge reservoir of solar power: One half of all our energy from the sun hits the tropics. Since 90 percent of the tropical surface of the planet is water, 45 percent of all the energy the earth receives from the sun is thus handy and ready in the brightly hued waters of the equatorial ocean.

Secondly, there is a 32°F to 45°F difference between the hot surface water and the deep water in the tropics. In the Florida Current, for instance (which brings warm water past Miami from the Caribbean), the surface varies from 72.5°F to 80°F and at a depth of 1,000 feet the temperature is a steady 36°F.

The only obstacle to thermodynamic efficiency is the occurrence of certain upwellings that take place naturally. They bring up cold water from lower depths and thus disrupt the layered temperature differential which OTEC requires to work. One of these upwellings occurs in the Humboldt Current, which is hospitable to certain fish (hence the enormous anchovy catch off Peru).

Von Arx says we should limit the power taken off by this method to the level of today's world demand for energy—10^{13} watts. If we take any more, he warns, then the average sea temperature might drop one or two degrees centigrade. With that, he reports, we might be off to the races for renewed glaciation of the planet. This temperature drop might also inhibit the generation of thunderstorms and hurricanes in the tropics. Although their disappearance would eliminate some deaths, terror, and damage, it would also disturb the hydrology equilibrium—the geophysicist's way of saying it would reduce the area's water supply from rainfall—and thus upset agriculture and starve people.

ERDA's OTEC program, it seems to me, promises one fine new way of filling energy needs. The program involves an expenditure of $26 million the first year. Professor Heronemus thinks it will run to about $1 billion by the year of its completion in 1984. Heronemus is urging that the project be accelerated. I agree with him.

To examine in depth all the kinds of natural power listed would fill volumes of speculation. I devoutly hope this is being done by ERDA. Since we are interested here in energy's relationship to the environment I will touch briefly on only three more—photosynthesis, hydroelectric power, and tidal flow.

Photosynthesis is the process by which nature captures the energy of sunlight to produce carbon derivatives for protein, carbohydrates, and fats in the food chain. The energy transfer in photosynthesis on land totals an amount equal to the world's demand—10^{13} watts. But civilization profits from only about 1 percent—the rest (stalks, leaves, roots and husks) being discarded as rubbish and burned or buried in the ground, where some of it remains to fertilize the soil. The energy required to plant, harvest, process, package, and distribute food is ten times greater than the amount man ingests from the food itself, writes von Arx.[7] But, he suggests, by decomposing the wastes through anaerobic (oxygenless) digestion in closed containers, they could be made to yield methane and other gases with 10^{17} watts of power upon combustion. Animal manure, city sewage, garbage, and plankton from the ocean could also be reduced to methane gas and thus supply additional large loads of power. Anaerobic conversion of the two billion tons of domestic animal excreta would alone provide 10^{12} watts—sufficient to run all farm machinery. Very little of the power stored in biological tissues by photosynthesis, indirectly and directly, is flowing into tappable reservoirs at present. It represents another vast storehouse we can exploit with eco-sanity.

Several years ago the redoubtable Buckminster Fuller wrote a poem[8] in which he promised that an increase in hydroelectricity and other nonpolluting and nondepleting energy sources could end the world's population explosion. Apparently he had studied national statistics of all countries and detected an inverse correlation between the number of kilowatts available to a nation and its population growth rate. In other words, the lower the kilowatt total the higher the birthrate, and vice versa. The not-so-subtle inference was that when there's not enough electric light in the evening, people are left with no recourse but to make babies. Fuller proposed that the United States should increase its hydroelectric capability greatly and by intercontinental grids move enough kilowatts to China, India, and Africa so that, according to his analysis, we could reverse the population spirals in those areas.

Don't use fossil fuels to produce this electricity, he fumed, that's like drilling a hole in the vault of a bank to get dollar bills. Fuller was particularly keen on harnessing the fifty-three-foot tides in the Bay of Fundy.

The Canadian government will complete a $3 million feasibility study in 1978 on this possibility. Some estimates run as high as 10^{10} watts (13,000 megawatts) of power that could potentially be drawn through a series of dam ducts in the 145-mile-long bay.

Von Arx is not so sanguine about gravitation as a source of energy—the power of the "lunisolar tide," as he calls it. Despite the great hopes for the Bay of Fundy, he says about 10^{10} watts of tidal power are all there is worldwide, on a day-to-day basis.

But it is, oh, so clean and eco-harmless!

The same can't be promised for some Paul Bunyanesque designs (proffered by various inventive souls) for obtaining hydroelectric power from the Mediterranean and Red seas. These schemes are based on the high evaporation that takes place in those two basins. Each would gain power by the movement of water coming in from the Atlantic and Indian oceans as the evaporated water is replaced by the oceans. This movement is occurring right now. All that is necessary to put the first plan into effect is to place tidal mills at Gibraltar for the Mediterranean, and at Bab el Mandeb for the Red Sea. The mills could be hooked up to generators.

The second plan is more extraordinary: Dams would be erected to close off the two seas at Gibraltar, Suez, and Bab el Mandeb. Then the seas would be permitted to evaporate until their levels fall by about a hundred meters. This sequence would take some decades. Then dam gates could be opened to allow ocean water to pour through turbines to generate electricity—double the present world total of hydroelectric power.

The new low level of the seas would be maintained by admitting through the sluice gates only the number of gallons that is being evaporated in the seas. Thus a constant quantity of electric power through turbines could be assured—as with the plans for Qattara and the Dead Sea in chapter 3.

But there's an ecological stumbling block. It would derive from the Red Sea's position in the East African Rift. This continental valley suffers from what might be described as seismic indigestion, with stomach rumbles under the earth's crust. Since the skin is fractured and weak along that stretch, removing the weight of a 100 meters' depth of Red Sea water might be enough to release volcanic forces from beneath, and might set off earthquakes.

Nuclear power must be mentioned here, since it appears on every comprehensive list of the energy options that are offered to end America's shortage. But already some qualified observers are saying that nuclear power is a kind of technology whose future is past. This is astounding news to us who witnessed the first atom bomb of 1945, followed by the Atoms for Peace program of President Eisenhower; the first power plant at Shippenport, Pennsylvania, in the fifties; the sharing of nuclear facilities with friends and hangers-on abroad; the international demonstration of the first commercial nuclear ship *Savannah;* and finally the effort to transform the powering of United States naval vessels from fossil fuel burners to reactors.

Without setting forth in exhaustive detail why it is that this once bright star of the future may already be fading, I will summarize the reasons for its fall from popularity. To begin with, nuclear power has not proven as cost-competitive as once hoped. Second, there is a fresh fear that plutonium, especially as generated anew in the emerging fast-breeder reactors, will make it more difficult than ever to prevent irresponsible terrorists from building a cheap bomb and blackmailing whole nations. It has become so simple to

construct nuclear weaponry that a Princeton University undergraduate recently wrote a reliable and workable how-to-do-it plan
for building an atomic bomb at a cost of $2,500.[9] Third, the basic
uranium ore from which nuclear fuel is extracted and refined is in
limited supply.

Finally, the greatest deterrent to nuclear power's achieving the
dominance it was once headed for is an environmental one—
specifically, the so far hopeless task of safely storing or otherwise
disposing of radioactive wastes. Some radionuclides have a half-life
of 100,000 years. What a gift to leave our descendants! There is no
dependable airtight or watertight container that will last more than
a few years. So it still appears ultimately unsafe to stash the material underground.

As for sea storage, this has been done off the coast of the United
States (the practice has stopped now under the new Ocean Dumping Act) and off Cape Finisterre, France, by Europeans (it is to be
hoped that they have stopped too, pursuant to the Ocean Dumping Convention of 1973). Some United States fifty-gallon metal
drums with ends stuffed with concrete were searched for and
found by EPA's Robert Dyer in 1976 under 5,000 feet of water off
California, where they'd been left a few years earlier. The drums
had imploded and there was no trace of their lethal content.

This discovery is disturbing. The ocean's capacity to absorb
these wastes is definitely limited. Any nation secretly using international waters to dispose of them should recall Lady Macbeth of
Shakespeare's play crying, "Out, damned spot!" as she tried to
wash away the blood of her murdered husband, fearing that even if
she tried the ocean the red stain "would rather the multitudinous
seas incarnadine." With radioactive "spots" this fantasy could become death-dealing reality for all marine life—and for us humans
at the top of the food chain.

It has been suggested that as the tectonic plates slide one over
the other at the bottom of the sea, storage containers of wastes
might be automatically carried underneath and become part of the
molten magma, which is already radioactive. But this shouldn't be

counted on as a means of disposal, because radioactive wastes are far more intensely active than the magma, and they might be regurgitated volcanically later and contaminate the earth's surface, after all. Of course, the time frame involved in this sequence—thousands of years—would allow the radionuclides to decay, and some scientists think they would be harmless when finally spewed out by volcanoes. The conservative view is, Why take the chance?

The best and least complicated way to increase energy supplies right now is to cut down on wasteful practices—in agriculture, in manufacturing, and in the use of our vast numbers of power-using machines from autos, planes, ships, and trains to domestic appliances.

From these glances at present pluses and minuses of alternative energy uses, it should be apparent that good, safe sources beckon us to develop them, but that we must do so cautiously and always with an eye on the need to keep our activities in harmony with the earth, air, fire, and water about us.

Food Production

Another energy shortage—fuel for the body of man—has complex implications for the environment. To meet soaring demand for food to sustain the world's burgeoning population has already brought forth some inventive responses.

One of these is to use genetic techniques to breed man down in size, let's say to one tenth of his present height, just as if he had taken one of Alice in Wonderland's magic cakes. Then we could have smaller cars, doll-size houses, and eat only one tenth of the 1,000 pounds of food per year that we currently consume.

While we wait for all that to happen there are some more immediate paths to more food. Graham Molitor of the General Mills Corporation claims it's possible to accelerate photosynthesis by hyping it up with radioactive materials, to get as many as twelve crops per annum. Furthermore, he adds, with advanced fertilizers on hand now farmers can accomplish such an increase by tilling only half as much field space. Hence for a given acre it is now possible, he says, to increase present field yield by a factor of twenty-four.

If one or more of the projects for irrigating the deserts can be realized, and these speedups applied, there will be adequate potential farmland for feeding many times the present population. However, there are so many other reasons for stabilizing the number of human beings that one must pray more food will not automatically encourage parents everywhere to abandon birth control.

Farming the sea with revolutionary mariculture has been vigorously promoted by Howard Wilcox in his *Hothouse Earth*. He sees it as a means for producing more food with less heat than we get from present land-based, heat-intensive farming.

As a marine scientist who has headed the navy's ocean farm project, Wilcox convincingly portrays in his book how aquaculture can ultimately feed up to 200 billion people. Laying out nets to which sea plants would be attached and which would be anchored or held in place by wave-driven propellers—this would form the basic sea farm unit. Floating platforms would secure the nets from above.

Kelp and hundreds of other seaweeds have already proved susceptible of healthy growth in this artificial mode. Kelp is a truly efficient photosynthesizer, using solar energy suffused through the water. It can grow up to two feet a day, reaching lengths of 200 or more feet. The Japanese eat 100 million pounds of seaweed a year, according to Wilcox, and even in Western culture seaweed elements have been incorporated (Wilcox writes) in "sherbert, cheese, yogurt, chocolate milk, imitation coffee cream, custard, salad dressings, jellied candies, pie fillings, bread, butter mixes, pickled meats, meat pastes, sausage casings, preserves, frozen fruit, beer, candy and ice cream!"[10]

The kelp farm units would first be tested on the continental shelf, as the University of California is now doing. Later they could be multiplied and tied together in groups approaching the dimensions of the great land farms of the Midwest. Not only would they produce vast amounts of new vegetable matter as promised by Wilcox, but they would attract swarms of fish which could be harvested. Also they could be protected from overfishing by the presence of the floating platforms: Unauthorized fishing trawlers could hardly get at the fish directly under the farms without being noticed and kept out of the area by the crew on the platforms. These sea farms would have to be manned by aquaculturists living aboard the platforms, which would eventually become one form of the "city at sea" described earlier.

In summary, sea farming may provide more than enough food to prevent shortages, with no ill effect on the weather—you can hardly cause dust bowls at sea. But we hope such pleasing prospects will not reverse our efforts to cut population growth.

Environmental Modification
—Large-scale Projects

The big geomorphic proposals mentioned in chapter 4 are still pretty much on the drawing boards, or only glints in their creators' eyes. I hope they receive serious consideration by those who are in a position to give them momentum, particularly those projects whose environmental side effects appear to be benign.

I have to admit I'm titillated by the idea of Dr. O'Neill's colonies in space, despite their killing cost. If even a fraction of his fascinating plan gets under way it might uplift the spirit and purpose of our people, and those of other nations that participate. In Thoreau's felicitous phrase, "In the long run men hit only what they aim at."[11]

Weather Modification—Current Efforts to Cure the Western Drought

The 1977 western drought has revived somewhat the public's wish for broad-gauge weather control through cloud seeding. Washington's Governor Dixy Lee Ray has just signed a bill appropriating $125,000 for a three-month campaign to scatter dry ice and ammonium nitrate over the Cascade Mountains. The goal is more snow during the winter and, more to the point, water in the spring for Washington's billion-dollar wheat and fruit crops, which are menaced by a disastrous drought.

No new technical breakthroughs have arrived to supersede the technology described in chapter 1. Nor will one-shot deals be apt to make much progress. Long-term, deep research is needed both in atmospheric behavior and cloud seeding before any grand success stories can be expected.

As mentioned earlier, much legal trail-blazing must be done before the downwind implications of programs like Governor Ray's will be clear. Enraged cries of "cloud rustling" are now ringing in Idaho, where that state's officials charge that Washington is trying to purloin precipitation destined for the parched fields of Idaho. Until now even the giants of meteorology have to talk small when asked whether such accusations have any validity.

Environmental Warfare

Despite the pursuit by Senator Pell, of a treaty banning environmental war certain questions about our nation's security will remain as long as there is so little practical knowledge of environmental warfare. While our country continues to support the treaty, I would like to see our Department of Defense and CIA keep up research and monitoring in this field. First, we should be alert as to what may be going on abroad; and second, we should be ready with whatever defensive strategy our safety requires.

Pollution Control—Signposts Ahead

The impacts of man's yahoo habits on the environment have begun to moderate in parts of this country. Air and water are responding to cleanup schedules—for example, in some cities and in the Great Lakes.

Two quantum jumps in pollution control lie ahead, if citizens of all countries keep putting the pressure on their officials.

The first jump has been expressed by EPA scientists who say it's possible for engines of the future to achieve virtually complete consumption of whatever fuel they run on. When this occurs, no impurities will be emitted by engines because there will be no unburned fuel. Similarly, it is theoretically possible in manufacturing to process *all* of the raw materials into the end product, with no dirty effluent or slag left lying around; or else to recycle any of the waste products and use them elsewhere.

The second jump will happen when every nation develops as strong an Environmental Protection Agency as that of the United States is striving to be, and there is worldwide agreement on harmonized standards of environmental quality.

Climate—Worries over New Dust Bowls and Widening Desertification

There has been a clamor about climate during the winter of 1976–77. It has centered on two complaints: One has been the extreme cold in the eastern United States. Whatever the causes for it, they do not appear to be man-made nor fixable by man. The second has been on the widening drought in the states of Kansas, Oklahoma, Colorado, Arkansas, California, Washington, and Idaho, among others. The situation in the first four states is unique because of the recrudescence of the old dust bowl problem of the thirties. Once again dry topsoil is swirling around in the wind. Cultivation is hampered as dust storms blow up with ever greater frequency.

When the dust bowl catastrophe struck forty years ago, Franklin Delano Roosevelt's New Deal began the most ridiculed project of his long and controversial administration. It was the president's own idea. He called it "Shelterbelt." He wanted $75 million to plant trees along the windward borders of the farms affected, as a barrier against the wind, which was cutting away hundreds of tons of topsoil from plowed fields in the Great Plains. Congress balked, and he only got about $15 million. But Roosevelt kept the heat on and finally managed to get 217 million trees and shrubs planted between 1934 and 1942. They were laid out in strips, one after the other, on some 30,000 farms. These belts of trees stack up the wind on the windward side and cut down its velocity by 40 percent for a distance upwind roughly five times the height of the trees; downwind the speed is slowed by about 70 percent, and the effect continues for a distance equal approximately to forty-five times the height of the trees. Additional advantages are that these lines of trees trap snow, adding moisture to the farmland; attract birds; and generally spruce up the environment of the prairie.

In 1954 the United States Park Service found that 73 percent of the Roosevelt plantings were in fair to good condition. And the dust bowl had been replaced by viable farmland once more. By 1960 farmers were planting shelterbelts on their own: In North Dakota they planted 2,800 miles of these belts, about twice as many as in any one year under the New Deal program.[12]

Shelterbelts may be the savior of the seventies too, though they will take some hefty irrigation to get them started during the present drought—or some successful seeding of clouds, if the right kind show up.

As for the vast new areas of desert opening up in Africa, India, and South America, man appears to be the villain. He is clear-cutting jungles, particularly in Brazil, and overgrazing, slashing and burning, and letting too many people and goats onto land that was fragile to begin with. The United Nations Environment Program will hold a "desertification" conference in 1977 to pool knowledge and national wills in an attempt to reverse the march of sand.

Professor Smagorinsky of Princeton and NOAA is cautious about the ability of civilization to accomplish much more than peripheral improvement along the edges of deserts. Deserts *may* have been caused by such sins as overgrazing, he concedes, but he thinks large forces in the general circulation of the atmosphere aren't going to be changed by anything man does.

Growth—A Dirty Word?

The following story sums up the world's predicament on industrial-agricultural-economic growth: A Tunisian agricultural specialist was lecturing in a workshop session preparatory to the upcoming United Nations Conference on Desertification. Speaking about an area he had studied in his own country, the Tunisian pointed out that the place had too many people and animals, and to survive was going to have to drastically reduce the number of each. Whereupon an Upper Volta delegate banged his fist on the table and shouted, "Your solution is unacceptable in my country." (Its average income is less than $100 per capita and the population is slightly over one million.) "We want to enjoy growth like other countries and we plan to increase our population to thirty million!" The Tunisian replied coolly that he was talking about an agricultural problem and that his finding was based objectively on the facts of the matter. "What you are talking about," he continued, "is a matter for the politicians to decide. I am a scientist, not a politician.

The question of growth has been chewed over in every general environmental powwow of this decade. The doom-crying Club of Rome report of 1972 provides all the arguments against continuing growth at the present rate of increase in most of the industrial nations. I have touched on much of the unintended damage which overuse of the biosphere to achieve this growth inflicts on the environment, weather and climate. To avert more harm we will have to moderate the speed of our industrial machine, just as we have lowered the limit for autos to fifty-five miles per hour. Figuring out just what the equivalent of "fifty-five miles per hour" is in terms of gross national product will be accomplished only with much study, national and international agreement, and good will among the global citizenry.

Here is a tip that applies to all nations, both developed and undeveloped: Why not concentrate from now on not on quantity of output but on quality? Return to the craftmanship, both in making products and repairing them, that was once a nation's hallmark of success, before the Industrial Revolution began. Quality is labor-intensive, whether for manufacturing or for service industries; concentrating on quality might mitigate unemployment. This idea should be examined by economists and sociologists as well as manufacturers and service organizations. It might lead to a new philosophy and a change in life-style without which no nation, rich or poor, can turn away from the present addiction to nonstop industrial growth. The change won't come in this country until we finally have a presidential candidate who dares to run on a zero-growth platform.

I have said little about how our government should handle the emerging capacity of our civilization to control and change the environment in ways never before deemed possible. A law was passed in 1976 to develop a national policy on weather modification—a good step forward. Congress in still pondering refinements in our pollution control legislation. Meanwhile a popular first-term president is in the midst of moves to streamline the federal establishment. As his proposed Department of Energy would pull together all aspects of the energy problem, so a Department of Environment would do the same thing in the field of environment. Weather modification, pollution control, review of environmental impact statements, and protection of fish and wildlife now are all located in different corners of the government. Like severed parts of a snake, each is still twitching independently with little or no coordination. Since the environment is a complex but integrated mechanism of nature, so should the government's administrative dealings with it be orchestrated singly, under one command. The new department should include two brand-new functions: national land use management, and planning for control of urban transportation (vital because most city air pollution comes from cars, buses, and trucks). Environment, energy, and the related economic matters could then all be handled within the cabinet, with presidential attention to the major decisions. At the highest level, fair and reasonable trade-offs could be made to maintain both the health of our people and that of our economy.

"I'll bet you wonder why I called this meeting," has become a humorous but pertinent icebreaker when Washington officials get down to business. The reason I've raised all these complicated issues of environmental modification is that they concern us all and will become steadily more important to our future. Not many people understand more than one or two of the issues. Scientists have warmly encouraged this attempt to widen the circle of caring, comprehending citizens. Without an informed and active society that insists on good stewardship of our strange new powers, dangerous mistakes are bound to be made by government and we will all suffer.

In short, if we help our democracy to function properly we should have fair weather ahead.

NOTES

PREFACE

1. Fitzhugh Green, Sr., *The Romance of Modern Exploration,* No. 46 in Reading with a Purpose Series (Chicago: American Library Association, 1929), p. 31.

CHAPTER 1

1. Wilmot N. Hess, ed., *Weather and Climate Modification* (New York: John Wiley & Sons, 1974), p. 4.

2. Ibid., p. 5.

3. Ibid., p. 5.

4. Ibid., p. 12.

CHAPTER 2

1. B. J. Mason, *Clouds, Rain & Rainmaking,* second edition (Cambridge, England: Cambridge University Press, 1975), p. 133.

2. Ibid., p. 148.

3. Charles A. Lindbergh, *We* (New York and London: G. P. Putnam's Sons, 1927).

CHAPTER 3

1. Jules Verne, *The Purchase of the North Pole,* in Vol. 13, Works of Jules Verne, ed. Charles F. Horne (New York and London: F. Tyler Daniels Co., 1911).

2. Edward Teller, Wilson Talley, Gary H. Higgins, and Gerald W. Johnson, *The Constructive Uses of Nuclear Explosives* (New York: McGraw-Hill, 1968).

3. Maurice Ewing and William C. Donn, "A Theory of the Ice Ages" (Science, Vol. 123, No. 3207, June 15, 1956), pp. 1061–66.

4. Teller, et al., *The Constructive Uses of Nuclear Explosives.*

CHAPTER 4

1. E. M. Forster, "The Machine Stops," from *The Eternal Moment and Other Stories* (New York: The University Library, Grosset and Dunlap, 1964; copyright 1928, Harcourt, Brace & World).

2. Ibid.

3. Ibid.

4. William F. Buckley, *Saving the Queen* (New York: Doubleday & Co., 1976), p. 43.

5. I. N. Stroud, "Subterranea," a memorandum by Mr. Stroud from P. O. Box 295, Ajar, California, 1961.

6. Henry David Thoreau, *Walden and Other Stories* (Garden City, N.Y.: International Collectors Library, 1970), p. 36.

7. W. H. Hudson, *Green Mansions* (New York: Dodd, Mead & Co., 1949).

8. Gerard K. O'Neill, *The High Frontier* (New York: William Morrow & Co., 1977).

CHAPTER 5

1. From Exodus 16, as given in Olive Pell, *Olive Pell Bible* (New York: Exposition Press, 1952), simplified form of King James version.

2. Gordon J. F. MacDonald, "Geophysical Warfare: How to Wreck the Environment," in *Unless Peace Comes,* Nigel Calder, ed. (New York: Viking Press, 1968).

3. Athelstan Spilhaus, *Our New Age,* cartoon series (Chicago: Hall Syndicate, February 26, 1961).

4. MacDonald, *Geophysical Warfare: How to Wreck the Environment.*

5. Ibid.

6. Paul Brodeur, "Microwaves," from *The New Yorker*, issues of December 13 and December 20, 1976.

7. Lowell Ponte, *The Cooling* (Englewood Cliffs, N.J.: Prentice-Hall, 1976), p. 172.

CHAPTER 6

1. Nelson Glueck, *Rivers in the Desert: A History of the Negev* (New York: Farrar, Straus & Cudahy, 1959).

2. Ibid., p. 7.

3. Massachusetts Institute of Technology, *Inadvertent Climate Modification: Report of the Study of Man's Impact on Climate* (Cambridge, Mass.: MIT Press, 1970).

4. Paul J. Crutzen, *Estimates of Variations in Total Ozone Due to Natural Causes and Human Activities* (*AMBIO*, Vol. 3, No. 6, 1974), pp. 201–10.

5. Ibid.

6. National Academy of Sciences, *Halocarbons: Environmental Effects of Chlorofluoromethane Release* (Washington, D.C., 1976), pp. 1–4.

7. Stephen H. Schneider, with Lynne E. Mesinow, *The Genesis Strategy: Climate and Global Survival* (New York: Plenum Press, 1976).

8. Wilmot N. Hess, ed., *Weather and Climate Modification* (New York: John Wiley & Sons, 1974).

9. Ibid., p. 710.

10. Howard A. Wilcox, *Hothouse Earth* (New York: Praeger Publishers, 1975).

11. Ibid., p. 99.

12. Massachusetts Institute of Technology, *Inadvertent Climate Modification*.

13. Hess, *Weather and Climate Modification*.

14. Jules Verne, *Purchase of the North Pole*, in Vol. 13, *Works of Jules Verne*, ed. Charles F. Horne (New York and London: F. Tyler Daniels Co., 1911).

15. Hess, *Weather and Climate Modification*.

16. Ponte, *The Cooling*.

17. Hess, *Weather and Climate Modification*.

18. William L. Boeck, "Meteorological Consequences of Atmospheric Krypton–85," *Science*, Volume 193, July 16, 1976.

CHAPTER 7

1. Rachel Carson, *Silent Spring* (Boston: Houghton Mifflin Co., 1962).

2. Bryan Silcock, "Exported Pollution: An Emerging Global Irritant," column in the *Washington Post*, May 3, 1977, p. A19.

3. Robert Poujade, *Ministère de l'Impossible* (Ministry of the Impossible) (Paris: Calmann-Lévy, 1975).

4. Marshall I. Goldman, *The Spoils of Progress: Environmental Pollution in the Soviet Union* (Cambridge, Mass.: MIT Press, 1972).

5. Woven through pages 172 and 173 are some language and thoughts from a series of six articles by the author, titled "Man's Impact on the Earth's Climate," which appeared March 1–6, 1976, in the *Providence* (R.I.) *Journal and Evening Bulletin*.

6. Nevil Shute, *On the Beach* (New York: William Morrow & Co., 1957).

7. D. H. Meadows, D. L. Meadows, J. Rauders, and W. W. Behrens, III, *The Limits to Growth: Report by the Club of Rome on the Human Predicament* (New York: Universe Books, 1972).

CHAPTER 8

1. Vincent J. Schaefer, "Some Problems Concerning Weather Control," paper presented before the Sixteenth Annual Nevada Water Conference, September 27 and 28, 1962, Carson City, Nevada, p. 1.

CHAPTER 9

1. William and Paul Paddock, *Famine, 1975!* (Boston: Little, Brown, 1967).

2. Gerald O. Barney, ed., *The Unfinished Agenda: The Citizens' Policy Guide to Environmental Issues, A Task Force Report Sponsored by the Rockefeller Brothers Fund* (New York: Thomas Y. Crowell Co., 1977), p. 35.

3. Meadows, et al., *The Limits to Growth*.

4. William S. Von Arx, "Energy: Natural Limits and Abundances," *EOS* (American Geophysical Union, Washington, D.C.), Vol. 55, No. 9, September 1974, pp. 828–32.

5. Wilcox, *Hothouse Earth*.

6. Richard Greely, *Energy Use and Climate: Possible Effects of Using Solar Energy Instead of "Stored" Energy*, Mitre Corporation, McLean, Virginia, April 1975.

7. Von Arx, "Energy: Natural Limits and Abundances."

8. Buckminster Fuller, "A Poem by Buckminster Fuller," sent as a telegram to Senator Edmund S. Muskie of Maine, published on "Op Ed" page of *New York Times*, March 27, 1971.

9. John Aristotle Phillips, "The Fundamentals of Atomic Bomb De-

sign: An Assessment of the Problem of and Possibilities Confronting A Terrorist Group on Non-Nuclear Nations Attempting to Design a Crude PO–239 Fission Bomb," undergraduate paper, Princeton University, 1976.

10. Wilcox, *Hothouse Earth*.

11. Thoreau, *Walden* (section on Economy).

12. The three preceding paragraphs contain information from Arthur H. Carhart, "Shelterbelts: A Failure that Didn't Happen," *Harper's Magazine*, October 1960.

BIBLIOGRAPHY

Altshuller, Dr. Aubrey P., Testimony before the Subcommittee on the Environment and the Atmosphere, Committee on Science and Technology, House of Representatives, May 22, 1975.

Alyea, Fred N.; Cunnold, Derek M.; and Prinn, Ronald G., "Stratospheric Ozone Destruction by Aircraft-Induced Nitrogen Oxides," *Science,* Vol. 188, April 11, 1975, pp. 117–22.

Barney, Gerald O., ed., *The Unfinished Agenda: The Citizens' Policy Guide to Environmental Issues, A Task Force Report Sponsored by the Rockefeller Brothers Fund,* Thomas Y. Crowell Co., New York, 1977.

Beltzer, Klaus, ed., *Living with Climatic Change,* Proceedings of Toronto Conference Workshop November 17–22, 1975, Science Council of Canada. Ottawa, 1976.

Boeck, W. L., "Meteorological Consequences of Atmospheric Krypton–85," *Science,* Vol. 193, July 16, 1976.

Brewer, Sam Pope, "Study Says Man Alters Climate: UN Report Links Melting of Polar Ice to His Activities," *New York Times,* September 23, 1973.

Brosset, Cyrill, "Air-Borne Acid," *AMBIO* (Royal Swedish Academy of Science, Oslo, Norway), Vol. 2, No. 1–2, 1963, pp. 2–9.

Bryson, Reid A., "World Food Prospects and Climatic Change," Testimony to joint meeting of Senate Subcommittee on Foreign Agricultural Policy and Subcommittee on Agricultural Production, Marketing, and Stabilization of Prices of the Senate Agriculture Committee, October 18, 1973.

Buckley, William F., *Saving the Queen*, Doubleday & Co., New York, 1976.

Budyko, M. I., "The Future Climate," *EOS* (American Geophysical Union, Washington, D.C.) Vol. 53, No. 2 (October 1972) pp. 868–74.

Calder, Nigel, *The Weather Machine*, Viking Press, New York, 1975.

Carhart, Arthur H., "Shelterbelts: A 'Failure' That Didn't Happen," *Harper's Magazine*, October 1960.

Carson, Rachel, *Silent Spring*, Houghton Mifflin Co., Boston, 1962.

Carter, Luther, "Weather Modification: Colorado Heeds Voters in Valley Dispute," *Science*, Vol. 181, June 29, 1973, pp. 1347–50.

Changnon, Stanley A., Jr., "A Review of Inadvertent Mesoscale Weather and Climate Modification and Assessment of Research Needs," paper presented at Fourth Conference on Weather Modification, November 18–21 1974, at Fort Lauderdale, Florida, sponsored by American Meteorological Society, Boston, Massachusetts.

————, "Weather Modification in 1972: Up or Down?" *Bulletin of the American Meteorological Society*, Vol. 54, No. 7, July 1973, pp. 642–60.

————, *1971 Operational Report for METROMEX*, University of Chicago Press, Urbana, Illinois, 1971.

Commoner, Barry, *The Closing Circle*, Alfred A. Knopf, New York, 1971.

Crutzen, Paul J., "Estimates of Possible Variations in Total Ozone Due to Natural Causes and Human Activities," *AMBIO* (Royal Swedish Academy of Science, Oslo, Norway), Vol. 3, No. 6, 1974.

Curry-Lindahl, Kai, *Conservation for Survival*, William Morrow & Co., New York, 1972.

De Onis, Juan, "Oil Money May Make the Mideast Deserts Bloom," *New York Times*, October 23, 1974.

"Do Cities Change the Weather?" *Mosaic* (National Science Foundation, Washington, D.C.), Vol 5, No. 3, Summer 1974, pp. 29–34.

Dorschner, John, "Look Out! Here Comes the Sahara," *Tropic*, December 29, 1974.

Dotto, Lydia, "Scientists Seek Treaty on Weather Triggers: Key to Military, Economic Power," *Globe and Mail*, Toronto, Canada, December 12, 1974.

Droessler, Earl G., "Weather Modification, Review and Perspective,"

Bulletin of the American Meteorological Society, April 1972, pp. 345–48.

Dugan, James; Cowen, Robert C.; Barada, Bill; and Crum, Richard M., *World Beneath the Sea*, National Geographic Society, Washington, D.C., 1967.

Eckholm, Erik P., *Losing Ground: Environmental Stress and World Food Prospects*, W. W. Norton & Co., New York, 1976.

Ehrlich, Paul R., *The Population Bomb*, Ballantine Books, New York, 1971.

Ewing, Maurice, and Donn, William C., "A Theory of the Ice Ages," *Science*, Vol. 123, No. 3207, June 15, 1956, pp. 1061–66.

Falk, Richard A., "Environmental Warfare and Ecocide—Facts, Appraisal, and Proposals," *Bulletin of Peace Proposals*, Oslo, 1973.

Federal Council for Science and Technology, Council on Environmental Quality, *Report of Federal Task Force on Inadvertent Modification of the Stratosphere: Flourocarbons and the Environment*, U.S. Government Printing Office, Washington, D.C., 1975, Library of Congress catalog number 75600057.

Federal Council for Science and Technology, *First Annual Report of Ad Hoc Committee on Geodynamics*, USIGP–F476, Washington, D.C., 1976.

———, *Report of the Ad Hoc Panel on the Present Interglacial*, ICAS 1Eb–FY75, Washington, D.C., August 1974.

Finney, John W., "Pentagon Replies on Peril to Ozone," *New York Times*, October 16, 1974.

Fleagle, Robert G.; Crutchfield, James A.; Johnson, Ralph W.; and Abdo, Mohamed F., *Weather Modification in the Public Interest*, University of Washington Press, Seattle, 1974.

Forster, E. M., "The Machine Stops," from *The Eternal Moment and Other Stories*, Universal Library, Grosset & Dunlap, New York, 1964; copyright 1928, Harcourt, Brace & World.

Freeman, Peter, *Coastal Zone Pollution by Oil and Other Contaminants: Guidelines for Policy, Assessment and Monitoring in Tropical Regions, Based upon a Case Study in Indonesia in 1973*, Office of International and Environmental Programs, Smithsonian Institution, Washington, D.C., 1974.

———, *The Environmental Impact of a Large Tropical Reservoir: Guidelines for Policy and Planning, Based upon a Case Study of Lake Volta, Ghana, in 1973 and 1974*, Office of International and Environmental Programs, Smithsonian Institution, Washington, D.C., 1974.

———, *The Environmental Impact of Rapid Urbanization: Guidelines for*

Policy and Planning, Based upon a Case Study of Seoul, Korea, in 1972 and 1973, Office of International and Environmental Programs, Smithsonian Institution, Washington, D.C., 1974.

Fuller, Buckminster, "A Poem by Buckminster Fuller," sent as a telegram to Senator Edmund Muskie of Maine, published on "Op Ed" page of *New York Times,* March 27, 1971.

Glueck, Nelson, *Rivers in the Desert: A History of the Negev,* Farrar, Straus & Cudahy, New York, 1959.

Goldman, Marshall I., *The Spoils of Progress: Environmental Pollution in the Soviet Union,* MIT Press, Cambridge, 1972.

Gosnell, Marianna, "Ozone—The Trick Is Containing It Where We Need It," *Smithsonian,* June 1975.

Granger, Bruce Ingham, *Benjamin Franklin: An American Man of Letters,* Cornell University Press, Ithaca, New York, 1964.

Grant, Lewis O., and Reid, John D., *Workshop for an Assessment of the Present and Potential Role of Weather Modification in Agricultural Production,* Atmospheric Science Department, Colorado State University, 1975.

Greely, Dr. Richard, *Energy Use and Climate: Possible Effects of Using Solar Energy Instead of "Stored" Energy,* Mitre Corporation, McLean, Virginia, April 1975.

Green, Fitzhugh, Sr., *The Romance of Modern Exploration,* No. 46 in Reading with a Purpose Series, American Library Association, Chicago, 1929.

Green, Fitzhugh, "Man's Impact on the Earth's Climate," six articles in the *Providence* (R.I.) *Journal and Evening Bulletin,* March 1–6, 1976.

Gribbin, John, "Weather Warning: You Are Now Experiencing a Climatic Change," *Nature,* Vol. 252, November 15, 1974.

Hammond, Allen L., "Modeling the Climate: A New Sense of Urgency," *Science,* Vol. 185, September 27, 1974, pp. 1145–47.

———, "Weather and Climate Modification: Progress and Problems," *Science,* Vol. 181, August 17, 1973, pp. 644–45.

Hard, Thomas M., and Broderick, Anthony J., eds., *Proceedings of the Fourth Conference on the Climatic Impact Assessment Program,* sponsored by the U.S. Department of Transportation, Department of Transportation Report No. DOT–TSC–OST–75–38, Washington, D.C., February 1976.

Harrison, Gordon, *Earthkeeping: The War with Nature and a Proposal for Peace,* Houghton Mifflin Co., Boston, 1971.

Heilbroner, Robert L., *An Inquiry into the Human Prospect,* W. W. Norton & Co., New York, 1974.

Hess, Wilmot N., ed., *Weather and Climate Modification*, John Wiley & Sons, New York, 1974.

Hobbs, P. V.; Harrison, H.; and Robinson, E., "Atmospheric Effects of Pollutants: Pollutants Which Affect Clouds Are Most Likely to Produce Modification in Weather and Climate," *Science*, Vol. 183, No. 4128, March 8, 1974, pp. 909–15.

House Committee on Foreign Affairs, Subcommittee on International Organizations and Movements, Hearings: *Weather Modification as a Weapon of War, September 24, 1974*, U.S. Government Printing Office, Washington, D.C.

House Committee on Science and Technology, Subcommittee on the Environment and the Atmosphere, Hearings: *National Climate Program Act, May 18–20 and 25–27, 1976*, U.S. Government Printing Office, Washington, D.C.

Hudson, W. H., *Green Mansions*, Dodd, Mead & Co., New York, 1949.

Huff, F. A., and Changnon, S. A., Jr., "Climatological Assessment of Urban Effects on Precipitation at St. Louis," *Journal of Applied Meteorology*, Vol. 11, August 1972, pp. 823–42.

———, "Precipitation Modification by Major Urban Areas," *Bulletin of the American Meteorological Society*, Vol. 54, No. 12, December 1973, pp. 1220–32.

Hughes, Patrick, *American Weather Stories*, National Oceanic and Atmospheric Administration Environmental Data Service, Washington, D.C., 1976.

International Federation of Institutes for Advanced Study, "Statement of IFIAS on Climate Change and World Food Production," Boulder, Colorado, October 3, 1974.

Jeffery, William P., Jr., *Unless . . .* , Dodd, Mead & Co., New York, 1975.

Joffe, Joyce, *Conservation: Interdependence in Nature*, Aldus Books, London, 1969.

Kahn, Herman; Brown, William; and Martel, Leon (with the assistance of the staff of the Hudson Institute), *The Next 200 Years: A Scenario for America and the World*, William Morrow & Co., New York, 1976.

Kellogg, W. W., and Schneider, Stephen H., "Climate Stabilization: For Better or for Worse?" *Science*, Vol. 186, No. 4170, December 27, 1974, pp. 1163–72.

King, Seth S., "Sun Cycle Indicates Severe Drought in '76," *New York Times*, May 21, 1975.

Ladurie, Emmanuel Le Roy, *Times of Feast, Times of Famine*, Doubleday & Co., Garden City, New York, 1971.

Landsberg, Helmut, and Machta, Lester, "Anthropogenic Pollution of the Atmosphere: Where To?" *AMBIO* (Royal Swedish Academy of Science, Oslo, Norway), Vol. 3, No. 3–4, October 1974, pp. 146–50.

Landsberg, Helmut E., "Man-Made Climatic Changes," *Science*, Vol. 170, December 18, 1970, pp. 1265–74.

Likens, Gene E. and Bormann, F. Herbert, "Acid Rain: A Serious Regional Environmental Problem," *Science*, Vol. 184, pp. 1176–79.

Lynn, Isabelle, "Whither Weather?" *National Parks and Conservation Magazine*, Vol. 48, No. 2, February 1974, pp. 14–15.

McHarg, Ian L., *Design with Nature*, Natural History Press, Garden City, New York, 1969.

MacDonald, Gordon J. F., "Geophysical Warfare: How to Wreck the Environment," in *Unless Peace Comes*, Nigel Calder, ed., Viking Press, New York, 1968.

MacLeish, William H., ed., *Oceanus*, Vol. 18, No. 4, Summer 1975.

Mason, B. J., *Clouds, Rain and Rainmaking*, second edition, Cambridge University Press, Cambridge, England, 1975.

Massachusetts Institute of Technology, *Inadvertent Climate Modification: Report of the Study of Man's Impact on Climate*, MIT Press, Cambridge, Mass., 1971.

———, *Man's Impact on the Global Environment: Assessment and Recommendations for Action, A Report of the Study of Critical Environmental Problems*, MIT Press, Cambridge, Mass., 1970.

Meadows, D. H.; Meadows, D. L.; Rauders, J.; and Behrens, W. W., III, *The Limits to Growth: Report by the Club of Rome on the Human Predicament*, Universe Books, New York, 1972.

Menon, P. K., "Modifying the Weather: A Story Issue," *New York Times*, Letters to the Editor, August 10, 1972.

Mitchell, Dr. J. Murray, Jr., "A Reassessment of Atmospheric Pollution as a Cause of Long-Term Changes of Global Temperature," from Singer, S. Fred, ed., *The Changing Global Environment*, D. Reidel Publishing Co., Dordrecht, Holland, 1975.

———, "Is Man's Industry Upsetting World Weather?" (reprint), *ESSA World* (U.S. Department of Commerce, Environmental Science Services Administration, Washington, D.C.), Vol. 3, No. 4, October 1968.

———, "The Weatherman Ponders the Future," *Wellesley Alumnae Magazine*, Vol. 49, No. 5, July 1965.

———, "Some Reflections on Environment and Society," President's Column, *Junior League Newsletter*, Winter 1971–72.

———, "Summary of Climate Modification Risk to Fossil Fuel Utilization, Pollution," and "Climate Modification Risk," excerpted from *Proceedings of Quantitative Environmental Comparison of Coal and Nuclear Electrical Generation and Their Associated Fuel Cycles Workshop*, Vol. 1, Mitre Technical Report No. MTR–7010, Contract Sponsor: National Science Foundation, NSF C925, 173c, W52, August 1975.

————, "What Can We Say About Future Trends in Our Climate?" in *Atmospheric Quality and Climatic Change: Papers of the Second Carolina Geographical Symposium, 1975*, Richard S. Kopec, ed., Studies in Geography No. 9, Department of Geography, University of North Carolina at Chapel Hill, 1976.

————, "World Climate: Major Changes Under Way?" *NOAA* (quarterly publication of National Oceanic and Atmospheric Administration, Washington, D.C.), Vol. 5, No. 2, April 1975.

Mordy, Wendell A., "Who's Changing the Weather?", *Center Report*, (Center for the Study of Democratic Institutions, Santa Barbara, Cal.), Vol. 6, No. 4, October 1973, pp. 7–10.

"NAS Warning on Climate Changes," *Science News*, Vol. 107, January 25, 1975.

National Academy of Sciences, *The Atmospheric Sciences and Man's Needs: Priorities for the Future*, Washington, D.C., 1971.

————, Assembly of Mathematical and Physical Sciences, Committee on Impacts of Stratospheric Change, *Halocarbons: Environmental Effects of Chlorofluoromethane Release*, Washington, D.C., 1976.

————, National Research Council, Committee on Atmospheric Sciences, *Weather and Climate Modification: Problems and Progress*, Washington, D.C., 1973.

National Science Foundation, *Weather and Climatic Change: Report of the Special Commission on Weather Modification*, NSF–66–3, Washington, D.C., 1965.

North American Interstate Weather Modification Council, Its Purposes and Activities, Office of the NAIWMC, Las Cruces, New Mexico, Publication No. 76–2 September 1976.

Nyberg, Alf, *On Transport of Sulphur over the North Atlantic*, Swedish Meteorological and Hydrological Institute, 1976.

O'Neill, Gerard K., *The High Frontier*, William Morrow & Co., New York, 1977.

————, "Space: A Place in the Sun," *New York Times*, June 12, 1975.

O'Toole, Thomas, "Ozone Shield Is Shrinking," *Washington Post*, December 12, 1974.

Paddock, William and Paul, *Famine, 1975!*, Little, Brown and Co., Boston, 1967.

"A Way to Change Weather?", *Pekin Times*, December 26, 1974, reported in UPI story.

Pell, Claiborne, with Harold L. Goodwin, *Challenge of the Seven Seas*, William Morrow & Co., New York, 1966.

Pell, Olive, *Olive Pell Bible*, Crown Publishers, Inc., New York, 1952. Library of Congress catalog number 52–6097.

Peterson, James T. and Flowers, Edwin C., *Urban-Rural Solar Radiation and Aerosol Measurements in St. Louis and Los Angeles, Symposium on Atmospheric Diffusion and Air Pollution, Santa Barbara, California, September 9–13, 1974*, American Meteorological Society, Boston, pp. 129–31.

Phillips, John Aristotle, "The Fundamentals of Atomic Bomb Design. An Assessment of the Problem of and Possibilities Confronting a Terrorist Group on Non-Nuclear Nations Attempting to Design a Crude PO–239 Fission Bomb" (undergraduate paper), Princeton University, 1976.

"Policy Statement of the American Meteorological Society on Purposeful and Inadvertent Modification of Weather and Climate," *Bulletin of the American Meteorological Society*, Vol. 54, No. 7, July 1973, pp. 694–95.

Polk, Peggy, "Demands for Energy May Affect Climate," *St. Louis Post-Dispatch*, October 12, 1971.

Ponte, Lowell, *The Cooling*, Prentice-Hall, Inc., Englewood Cliffs, N.J., 1976.

Poujade, Robert, *Ministère de l'Impossible* (Ministry of the Impossible), Calmann-Levy, Paris, 1975.

Quarles, John, *Cleaning Up America*, Houghton Mifflin Co., Boston, 1976.

Randall, Judith, "Tinkering With Weather: Consequences Clouded," *Washington Star*, December 30, 1974.

Reston, James, "Battle for the Oceans," *New York Times*, March 21, 1975.

St. Amand, P.; Reed, D. W.; Wright, T. L.; and Elliott, S.D., "Gromet II: Rainfall Augmentation in the Philippine Islands," Naval Weapons Center, China Lake, California, May 1971.

Schaefer, Vincent J., "Some Problems Concerning Weather Control," paper presented at the Sixteenth Annual Nevada Water Conference, September 27 and 28, 1962, Carson City, Nevada.

Schneider, Stephen H., with Lynne E. Mesinow, *The Genesis Strategy: Climate and Global Survival*, Plenum Press, New York, 1976.

———, "The Population Explosion," *AMBIO* (Royal Swedish Academy of Science, Oslo, Norway), Vol. 3, No. 3–4, 1974, pp. 150–55.

Senate Committee on Foreign Relations, Subcommittee on Oceans and

International Environment, Hearings: *Prohibiting Military Weather Modification, July 26 and 27, 1972*, U.S. Government Printing Office, Washington, D.C.

————, Hearings: *Weather Modification, January 25 and March 20, 1974*, U.S. Government Printing Office, Washington, D.C.

Sewell, W. R. Derrick, ed., *Human Dimensions of Weather Modification*, Department of Geography Research Paper No. 105, University of Chicago Press, Chicago, 1966.

Shute, Nevil, *On the Beach*, William Morrow & Co., New York, 1957.

Sierra Club, *Air, Water, Earth, Fire: The Impact of the Military on World Environmental Order*, International Series 2, San Francisco, May 1974.

Silcock, Bryan, "Exported Pollution: An Emerging Global Irritant," *Washington Post*, May 3, 1977, p. A19.

Silverberg, Robert, *The Challenge of Climate*, Meredith Press, New York, 1969.

Simpson, Joanne, *The Global Energy Budget and the Role of Cumulus Clouds: Based on a series of five lectures given at a NATO Advanced Study Conference on the Air-Sea Boundary Layer, Ramsey, Isle of Man, September 21–October 2, 1970*, U.S. Department of Commerce, National Oceanic and Atmospheric Administration, Environmental Research Labs, NOAA Technical Memorandum ERL WMPO–8, November 1973.

Simpson, R. H., and Simpson, Joanne, "Why Experiments on Tropical Hurricanes?", *Transactions of the New York Academy of Sciences*, Ser. 22, Vol. 28, No. 8, June 1966, pp. 1045–62.

Simpson, R. H., "On the Design and Evaluation of Tropical Cyclone Seeding Experiments," paper presented at WMO Conference on Weather Modification, Manila, Philippines, 1974.

Soleri, Paolo, *The Bridge Between Matter and Spirit Is: Matter Becoming Spirit*, Anchor Books (Doubleday & Co.), Garden City, N.Y., 1973.

————, *Arcology: The City in the Image of Man*, MIT Press, Cambridge, Mass., 1969.

Southern, R. L., "Utilization of Tropical Cyclone Warning—Can Man Respond to Scientific Progress?" paper presented at the Australian Academy of Sciences Symposium on Natural Hazards in Australia, Canberra, May 26–29, 1976.

"Soviets Cite Perils of Weather War," *Washington Post*, October 23, 1974.

Spilhaus, Athelstan, *Our New Age*, cartoon series, Hall Syndicate, Chicago, February 26, 1961.

Stanford, Philip, "Is the Pentagon Tinkering Too Much with the Weather?", *Parade*, May 4, 1975, p. 23.

Stewart, Harris B., Jr., *The Global Sea*, D. Van Nostrand Co., 1963.

Stockholm and Beyond, Report of the Secretary of State's Advisory Committee on the 1972 United Nations Conference on the Human Environment, May 1972. GPO No. 0-463-237.

Straub, Conrad P., ed., *Critical Reviews in Environmental Control*, CRC Press, Cleveland, 1975.

Stroud, John M., "Subterranea," an unpublished memorandum by Mr. Stroud (a consultant) to Mr. J. W. Sigford of the Minneapolis-Honeywell Company, Minneapolis, Minn., November 8, 1961. Questions can be addressed to Mr. Stroud, P.O. Box 5065, Ojai, California 93023.

Suits, C. Guy, ed., *The Collected Works of Irving Langmuir:* Vol. 12, *Langmuir, the Man and the Scientist*, Pergamon Press, New York, 1962.

Sullivan, Walter, "Deep-Drilling Projects on Coast Envisions Probes into Molten Interior and Fault Zone," *New York Times*, June 12, 1975.

———, "Quakes on West Coast Linked to 'Lubrication,' " *New York Times*, June 3, 1975.

———, "Scientists Ponder Why World's Climate Is Changing," *New York Times*, May 21, 1975.

———, "Vast Antarctic Ice Sheet Studied for Clues to Periodic Ice Ages," *New York Times*, May 22, 1975.

Tanaka, Kakuei, *Building A New Japan*, translated by Simul International, Simuls Press, Inc., Tokyo, 1972.

Taubenfeld, Rita F., and Taubenfeld, Howard J., "The International Implications of Weather Modification Activities," U.S. Department of State, Office of External Research, June 1968.

Teller, Edward; Talley, Wilson; Higgins, Gary H.; and Johnson, Gerald W., *The Constructive Uses of Nuclear Explosives*, McGraw-Hill, New York, 1968.

Thomas, William L., Jr. ed., *Man's Role in Changing the Face of the Earth*, University of Chicago Press, Chicago, 1956.

Thoreau, Henry David, *Walden and Other Stories*, International Collectors Library, Garden City, N.Y., 1970.

"Threat to Ozone Called Peril To Life," *Chicago Sun-Times*, December 12, 1974.

Toffler, Alvin, *Future Shock*, Bantam Books, New York, 1971.

Tribus, Myron, "Physical View of Cloud Seeding," *Science*, Vol. 168, No. 3928, April 10, 1970, pp. 201-11.

United Nations General Assembly, Twenty-ninth Session, *First Committee Record of Meeting re Weapons*, October 1974, and *Prohibition of Action to Influence the Environment and Climate for Military and Other Purposes Incompatible with the Maintenance of International Security, Human Well-Being and Health*, December 1974.

U.S. Arms Control and Disarmament Agency, Press Releases: "Second Round of Environmental Modification Talks Conclude—Joint U.S.–U.S.S.R. Release" and "Environmental Warfare Talks Begin," July 3, 1974, and "Joint U.S.–U.S.S.R. Statement," November 5, 1974.

U.S. Department of Interior, Bureau of Reclamation: "Weather Modification Expert Joins Reclamation's Project Skywater," press release September 23, 1974.

U.S. Department of the Navy, Naval Weapons Center, Earth and Planetary Sciences Division, Research Department, *Handbook of Applied Weather Modification; Part 1. Cold Cloud Modification Subsystem, Volume 1 Cumulus Cloud Treatment*, NWC TP 5160, China Lake, California, February 1975.

Verne, Jules, *The Purchase of the North Pole*, in Vol. 13, *Works of Jules Verne*, ed. Charles F. Horne, F. Tyler Daniels Co., Inc., New York and London, 1911.

Von Arx, William S., "Energy: Natural Limits and Abundances," *EOS*, (American Geophysical Union, Washington, D.C.), Vol. 55, No. 9, September 1974.

———, *An Introduction to Physical Oceanography*, Addison-Wesley Publishing Co., Reading, Mass., 1962.

Weigel, Edwin P., "World Climate: Major Changes Under Way? A Distinguished Climatologist Discusses One of Our Greatest Enigmas," interview, Dr. J. Murray Mitchell, Jr., *NOAA* (quarterly publication at National Oceanic and Atmospheric Administration, Washington, D.C.), Vol. 5, No. 2, April 1975, pp. 16–21.

Weisbecker, Leo W., *Snowpack, Cloud-Seeding, and the Colorado River: A Technology Assessment of Weather Modification*, University of Oklahoma Press, Norman, 1973.

Weisman, Joel D., " '72 Flood Laid to Cloud Seeding: Suit Filed in Rapid City," *Washington Post*, June 3, 1975.

Westing, Arthur H., "Proscription of Ecocide: Arms Control and the Environment," *Science and Public Affairs*, Vol. 30, No. 1, January 1974, pp. 24–27.

Wilcox, Howard A., *Hothouse Earth*, Praeger Publishers, New York, 1975.

Wilkie, W. R., and Neal, A. B., "Meteorological Features of Cyclone

Tracy," paper presented at the Australian Academy of Sciences Symposium on Natural Hazards in Australia, Canberra, May 26–29, 1976.

Woodley, William L., and Sax, Robert I., *The Florida Area Cumulus Experiment: Rationale, Design, Procedures, Results, and Future Course,* National Oceanic and Atmospheric Administration Technical Report ERL 345–WMPO 6, U.S. Government Printing Office, Washington, D.C., 1976.

Zito, Tom, "Whither the Weather? The Answer Is Blowing in the Wind, Maybe," *Washington Post,* February 24, 1975.

INDEX

235